Contents

Art &
Design

for
learning

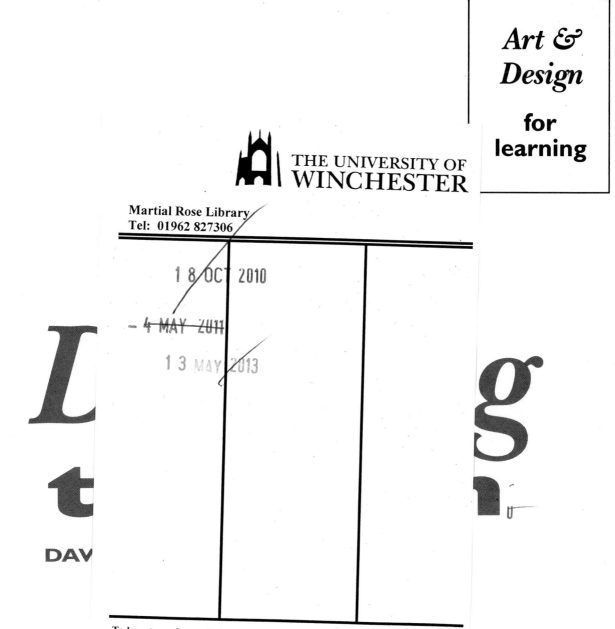

DAV

Hodder & Stoughton
LONDON SYDNEY AUCKLAND

British Library Cataloguing in Publication Data

Sedgwick, Dawn
   Drawing to Learn
   I. Title II. Sedgwick, Fred
   372.5

ISBN 0 340 57341 4

First published 1993
Impression number   10 9 8 7 6 5 4 3 2 1
Year   1998 1997 1996 1995 1994 1993

Typeset by Wearset, Boldon, Tyne and Wear
Printed in Great Britain for the educational publishing division of Hodder &
Stoughton Ltd, Mill Road, Dunton Green, Sevenoaks, Kent by Scotprint Ltd.

Series preface: Art and design for learning

Art and design for learning is a series of books which aims to provide a number of individuals involved in teaching with a platform from which to write about working with children and the thinking which lies behind their work.

The series authors are all experienced teachers and educationalists. They have had the privilege of visiting and working in schools, or of working with groups of teachers who have generously given permission for their children's work, and some of their own thoughts, to be included.

In the present climate of intense curriculum development created by the introduction of the National Curriculum for England and Wales, there is a great fear amongst some teachers that room for individuality and inventiveness is in danger of being lost. If this were to be the case, it would of course be disastrous but it need not happen.

Research historians and cooks experimenting with fifteenth- and seventeenth-century bread and cake recipes encountered failure until they realised that the key ingredient was never listed. This was because all the practitioners knew it to be such a basic necessity that everyone concerned would already know about it. The unlisted ingredient was yeast.

The same principle could be applied to many of our curriculum documents. The yeast in art and design education must surely be the life, energy and individuality of the child and the teacher, working creatively with the ingredient of experience and the means. Any defined curriculum agreed upon by others and presented to an establishment, an authority, county or state is inclined to appear restrictive at first glance, especially if we personally have not been responsible for drafting it. What we are able to do with it will depend on whether we see it as a platform to work from, or a cage to be imprisoned in.

It is therefore very important to coolly appraise the nature and content of the work we are undertaking with the children in our schools and to think carefully about our personal philosophy and values. We need to identify areas of any imposed curriculum that we are in fact already covering and then consider those which call for development or may need to be introduced. It is only when we really understand the common denominator which lies behind these areas of experience that we can assimilate them into a holistic and coherent developmental pattern on which to base our strategies for practice.

In simple terms any sound curriculum pertaining to art, craft and design must surely require a broad, balanced, developmental programme which has coherence and respects the experience, strengths, and weaknesses of individual children thereby enabling them to think, respond and act for themselves. Perhaps the real evaluation of a good teacher is to see whether children can proceed with their learning independently when he/she is no longer responsible for them.

The curriculum should make it possible to introduce children to the wonders and realities of the world in which we all live and should include art, craft and design forms from our own and other cultures and times. These can prove to be an enriching experience and can broaden the children's expectation of the nature of human response together with some experience of different ways of making art and design forms.

The curriculum should enable children to see the potential, and master the practice, of any relevant technologies: from the handling of simple hand tools to the world of information technology. It should enable them to work confidently in group and class situations as well as individually: thinking, making, appraising and modifying the work they are undertaking, negotiating skilfully with one another and discussing or talking about what they are doing, or have done. All of these aspects of education can be seen in the context of the National Curriculum which has, in the main, been based on some of the best practices and experience of work in recent years.

Intimations of the yeast component are clearly apparent in these selected extracts from *Attainment Targets and Programmes of Study for Key Stages 1 and 2*. (It is also very interesting to note the clear differences in requirements between the two stages; at seven- and at eleven-years-of-age. Stage 2 assimilates and develops Stage 1 requirements, building on them developmentally with specific additions.) At Key Stage 1 (seven-years) the operative words are:

> investigating, making, observing, remembering, imagining, recording, exploring, responding, collecting, selecting, sorting, recreating, recognising, identifying, *beginning* to make connections ... [my italics].

There is a very strong emphasis throughout on *direct experience, looking at* and *talking about*. At Key Stage 2 (eleven-years) the following expectations are added:

> communicating ideas and feelings, developing ideas, experimenting [there is a subtle difference between exploration and conscious experimentation], applying knowledge, planning and making, choosing appropriate materials, adapting and modifying, comparing, looking for purposes, discussing ...

What could be clearer in suggesting a lively educational experience? I believe that individuality and inventiveness are firmly based on having the right attitudes and they usually thrive best in the context of vehicles such as interest, happenings and the building up of enthusiasm and powerful motivation. The overall structure, balance and developmental nature of any sound curriculum model can allow content to flourish in lively interaction between children, teachers and the world of learning experiences.

If we persist in hardening the content of the National Curriculum in such a way that we are not able to manoeuvre or respond to the living moment, then we have ourselves forged the links of the chain which binds us.

The books in this series do not aim to be comprehensive statements about particular areas of art, craft and design experience but they are vigorous attempts to communicate something of the personal, convinced practice of a number of enthusiastic professionals. We hope that they will also offer enough information and guidance for others to use some of the approaches as springboards for their own exploration and experience in the classroom.

Preface

Drawing is an art in its own right. It can be done with the simplest and cheapest of materials and more than any of the other arts is accepted as the normal way of non-verbal communication.

(Philip Rawson, 1979)

Drawing to learn is a celebration of practical teaching and thinking on the part of the two authors based on their own experience and supported by teachers and children with whom they have worked. It is characterised by a strong personal conviction of the value of children's art and thinking, high expectation and a respect for creativity.

They are not alone in their belief that drawing is one of the most powerful means of learning, communicating and expressing that there is. It is not only non-verbal, it is pre-verbal and has its roots in intuitive and logical modes of thinking and acting. In the context of this book (as in many educational fields), drawing is broadly interpreted and where it naturally uses the tools and media, or develops into painting, collage or textiles for example, it has been given its head.

Drawing is mark-making, with every tool and material known to the human race: graphic tools, brushes, fingers, hands, imprinting, using modelling and cutting tools, threads, fibres, wire and whatever else is or ever has been available. Drawing is an attitude of mind, a form of enquiry; not an end in itself so much as a way of understanding, of seeing potential, or of using. Drawing deepens understanding through involvement, by utilising an intensity of looking, selecting, organising. . .

In the context of the National Curriculum drawing plays a key role. It would be simplistic and limiting to see it as a pencil precursor to painting, modelling or sculpture, because it is only when the child has sufficient experience of the qualities of these other materials that a graphic tool can be used as a shorthand, or as a planning device. Tight little clay heads, following tight little, hard pencil drawings, or painted drawings being considered as paintings, do little to enhance either media.

It is well worth looking at the National Curriculum requirements solely from a drawing standpoint. There are very few General, or End of Key Stage statements (supported by Programmes of Study) where it cannot play an important role.

The development of visual perception and the skills associated with investigating art, craft and design [is a major aspect, together with] recording observations, [and] responding to memory and imagination, . . . exploring the elements of art and ranges of tools and techniques.

(Key Stage 1 (seven-years-old), Attainment Target 1, *Investigating and Making*)

Similarly, Key Stage 2 includes: 'Selecting . . . , using. . . , applying what you have learned,' (together with further development and practice of the Key Stage 1 requirements). The programme of study introduces the children to the 'use of a sketchbook to record observations and ideas'.

There is nothing magic about a sketchbook unless it is seen for the value of its content, as a means to search and research and make preliminary notes and drawings rather than little end products. Preliminary studies and sequences of work should be seen for what they are, the roots and branches of the vine.

Key Stage 1 and 2 (Attainment Target 2) *Knowledge and Understanding*, offers a rich experience of the drawings and designs of the world's people, from drawings on cave walls to contemporary works and the study of methods and media, which in turn should inform the children's own work. The whole offers a threefold experience of personal involvement leading to original work, materials and means and the world of other people's creation. Philip Rawson, as well as starting our thinking, can offer apposite last words:

a well-developed language of marks can convey more about what is represented than any mere copy of appearances.

(Philip Rawson, 1979)

Margaret Morgan, Art Education Consultant

Acknowledgments

We would like to thank the following teachers, headteachers and advisers who have allowed us to reproduce the work which children have done with them:

Mary and Peter Moore; Bryan Knights; Vicki Muller; Sue Mortimer; Margaret Jackson; John Harvey; Hilary Birkin; Patricia Laws; Lorna Williamson; Annie Glen; Margo Barker; Ruth Plumb; Di Brendish; Phil Goulding; Duncan Allan; Anne Fletcher; Helen Rolfe; Mary Minchington; John Langdon; Eddie Casey; Margaret Cox; Val Cumberbirch; Lyn Wallace; Lynn Wright; Doreen Bartlett; Carolyne Price; Andrew Webber; H B Eliot; Julie Brewer; Brigida Martino.

We would also like to thank Ian Chance, Director of Wingfield Arts, Wingfield College, Stradbroke, Suffolk; and the artist Antony Maitland. Other artists who inspired work reproduced in this book include Emmanual Jegede, Winston Lewis and Saleem Arif.

We are grateful to Academic Press for permission to include the Nadia Chomyn drawings from the Bethlem Royal Hospital Archive and Museum, Beckenham, Kent.

We are also very grateful to children from the following schools whose work is represented:

Murrayfield CP; Downing CP; St Helen's CP; Tattingstone VCP; Sprites Junior and Belstead Special all in Ipswich. Also Fairfield Infants, Felixstowe and St Peter VCP and St Paul VCP, in Eye. Clare Middle; Gisleham Middle; and Beccles Middle all in Suffolk; Swing Gate First, Berkhamsted, Hertfordshire and Chaulden Infants, Hemel Hempstead, Hertfordshire.

We would also like to thank Margaret Morgan for her constant advice and her many ideas, for which the book is richer than it would otherwise have been. We have done our utmost to include in these acknowledgements everyone who has helped us but we do apologise if we have inadvertently left anyone out.

This book is dedicated to all the children we have taught, in gratitude for the moments of pleasure, excitement and learning which their work has given us.

Children who learn to look, learn to question, to discover and to understand... Looking absorbs, engages, calms and sensitises the learner... Art is a way of looking, seeing, questioning and discovering.

(Mary Newland and Maurice Rubens, 1984)

Do you have to be able to draw?

(Child to a teacher starting a drawing club)

1 Mark-making in the nursery and on the cave wall

MARK-MAKING, DECODING AND INTERPRETATION IN OUR SCHOOLS

Think about communication. The first act of the human race was to *make* a mark, not to interpret one.

This may sound like a statement of the obvious. After all, how could anyone interpret a mark until one was made? We both like to imagine a drawing on a cave wall: a roughly-made boar perhaps, with a spear sticking out of it and two humans staring at this drawing with comically puzzled expressions. These two humans know who made this mark because of something in the style of the artist's line, the way a curve at the top end sweeps away to mean this is the work of... They know this drawing is telling them something and they have a dim idea of what it might be. They find in the backs of their minds some hint of the area it concerns: religion, food, celebrations, magic. Now the mark has been made, they have to puzzle it out, to interpret it. Is it a message saying 'We have killed'? Or is it a prayer that they might kill soon? Or a guarantee that they will?

But, conversely, with our children we treat reading (which is interpreting and decoding) as the primary act. So although our first paragraph may be a statement of the obvious, we seldom act as though it is in our schools. In these institutions we are more likely to act as though humankind was predominantly an interpreter. We seem to emphasise reading instead of drawing and writing. We put the interpretation of marks before the making of them.

This may well be because in a necessarily ordered society it is important that we learn how to read signs telling us what to do: *Drive on this side. Don't go there. It is forbidden to walk on the grass. Trespassers will be prosecuted. No Entry. Way Out.* Being able to interpret signs is a large part of being directed. This is not to say, of course, that reading isn't a vital part of our learning. It should go without saying that learning to read is the means by which we gain access to the traditions of the place where we find ourselves and also a way into understanding the wider world. It helps us to understand how others think and feel and leads us to look at other people's work.

But the more totalitarian societies become, the more they emphasise interpreting rather than making marks, because interpreting so often means being able to do what we are told, while marking means changing the world a little. When we mark, either by writing or drawing, we are in control. When we read (in the most simplistic sense of the word) we are controlled.

VALUING CHILDREN'S FIRST MARKS — A CHILD'S NEED FOR A POSITIVE ADULT RESPONSE

If we were to take a lesson from our prehistory, we would set more store as adults by our children's first marks, because we would understand how our race's first marks were so important. As the cave dwellers marked and considered their marks important (matters, indeed, of life and death) so children consider their marks important. We should respect our children's first drawings, those scribbles which, to us, look like so much litter at the end of another exhausting day of being a parent. It is so important to give very young children some confidence in their ability to make, to mark, to change the world a little.

We might also make a link between these marks and the children's language development. Paul Johnson argues in *Literacy through the Book Arts* (1992) that we all too readily divorce language from pictorial representation. He argues that drawing is not only the foundation for technical work in design later on but also the foundation for writing. A pivotal moment in our lives, which instigated a change of direction, occurred when an inspector said to one of us: 'There is splendid writing in this school and there is splendid drawing. Why do you always separate them?'

Why indeed? Mark-making, whether written or drawn, is the means by which we question and express our own views. Children need the opportunity to learn in whatever ways are open to them and with whatever materials we can offer them. That is why some of the drawings in this book have writing on them. The issue isn't about neatness; it's about learning. The best evidence of learning that we know of are Leonardo da Vinci's sketchbooks, which are full of notes (some in reverse writing), drawings and crossings out; a tumultuous mental activity conveyed in marks on the page.

Helen, the girl who made these drawings (see figures 1, 2, 3 below and pages 15 and 16) was between two- and four-years-of-age when she did them. What do they mean? How will her first writing and reading be affected by our responses to these marks? For example, we might say, 'Oh that's nice!' and pass on to something else, a conversation with an adult, for example, or a television programme, to which the child's eyes will wander, wonderingly: what is there that I've missed in my communication? Or we might simply ignore the drawings. Or we might say, 'Tell me about that.' Or we might frame it carefully and display it.

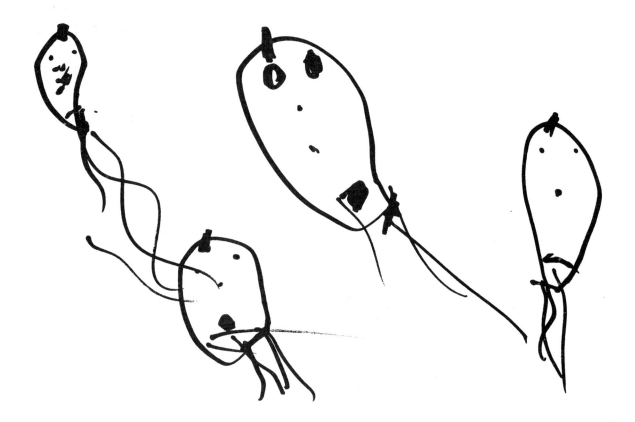

Figure I   *Mummy, Daddy, Helen and baby,* by girl aged three in felt-tip

We spoke to Helen's mother who had kept nearly all her daughter's drawings, framed them and put them on the wall.

You can see the development. There are a couple of really eerie ones, and maybe they show what she was thinking; when you're having another baby, for example... In one drawing [figure 1] she was about three, the round little figures look like lost souls. And she said, 'I'm lost and I'm saying help me, help me...' I don't like the ones I orchestrate! When you leave them alone they're the best ones ... their perceptions get on to the paper...

But although this mother stood back from her daughter's drawings, she had an active role in their creation. Unless she had encouraged, enabled, presented tools, time and space, Helen's work could not have been done. Helen's mother told us:

The first time she could see she was putting marks on the paper, when she could see she was responsible for it, she filled a piece of paper, every corner of it, learning she was in control of it. She really enjoyed it. She was about one.

(See *First Marks*, figure C1 on page 97 in the colour section, and figure C2 by another child of a similar age).

helen
21·3·88

Figure 2   *Cat*, by girl aged four in felt-tip

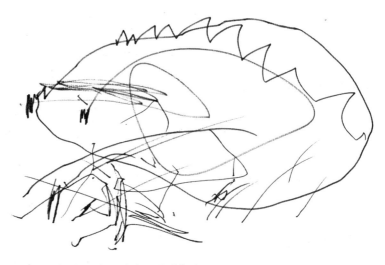

Figure 3 *Pig*, by girl aged three in felt-tip

She drew the pig (figure 3) when she was three-years-old. Already, simply because of the availability of materials and encouragement, her lines have a variety of depth and intensity that gives the piece vigour. There are also circles and zigzags, showing a willingness to experiment.

Later the same year Helen drew figure 1, *Mummy, Daddy, Helen and baby*, little spermatozoa-like creatures lost and sad on the large white card. Her mother was pregnant at the time with the baby depicted top left. She mentioned the open mouths to her daughter and it was then that she made the sad little remark about being lost. At four-years-of-age, she drew the little cat in figure 2. Note how her mother has not trimmed the paper and indeed the space in which the cat seems to be lost is eloquent.

CREATING AN ENVIRONMENT FOR MARK-MAKING

Before we begin to look at some work from a nursery, we would suggest that there must be an emotional and physical context in which we must function as teachers of drawing or indeed of any of the arts. It is crucial that children have the structure and security in school to be themselves and to know that what they think matters. We need relationships of mutual respect between teacher and pupil and an interesting and well-ordered physical environment, as well as appropriate tools and materials. We need to build into the setting the expectation that learners (adults as well as children) will explore and persevere, and that skills of many kinds will be used in the art lesson: listening and communicating as well as interacting in other ways.

FOCUS ON CHILDREN'S ART IN THE NURSERY

The following drawings (figures 4, 5 and 6) are by three, four-year-old Bangladeshi children who attend an English nursery school.

Figure 4 *African mask*, by boy aged four in white paint on black paper

These drawings suggest that children have their own artistic voice at a very early age. Artistic work with children with very little English is particularly worthwhile as it offers a valuable release for emotions which cannot be articulated and it is a means of communicating with other children. Drawing is after all a universal language.

The children had been looking at an African mask. The critical point about this work is that they have worked on a large scale. Too often drawing is seen as only a small-scale activity involving hard pencils and A4 paper. Here the paper is full-size sugar paper and the graphic tools are hoghair brushes.

Figure 5 *African mask, by girl aged four in charcoal*

Figure 6 *African mask, by girl aged four in charcoal, pencil and felt-tip*

Figure 7 *Person*, by girl aged four in felt-tip

Another significant feature of this work is that the children had been given an opportunity to work in white on black. Children need the chance to choose the colour of their paper as they need opportunities to choose everything else but their choices will only be informed if they have had the chance to work in different colours and tones before. Some children chose smaller paper, charcoal and black felt-tips or biros.

Figure 8 *Kulsuma wearing a sari*, by girl aged four in charcoal

This is kulsuma wearing a sari

Figure 9 *Dula*, by girl aged four in charcoal

The children had also been looking at art objects. Thus the learning is more than just practice with graphic tools, important though that is. It is learning about the way humankind has made art in the past and how it does so in the present. (We will discuss this further in Chapter 6.) To complement this contrast between art present and art past these four-year-olds were exposed to the power of art from a culture other than their own. All these factors contributed to the unusual vigour present in this work.

Nursery children (to use a category from *Art 4–11*, (Morgan, 1988)) are experimenting with materials and tools. In other words, if we let them, they explore. We can imprison them in narrow expectations, or we can allow them the uncertain and exciting processes of discovery. Their drawing at this stage is a symbolic interpretation based on holistic scanning and global vision. We can see this clearly illustrated in this work, by the white paint on black paper in figure 4 on page 17.

Morgan's categorisation of children's stages of development in art is worth quoting almost in full:

1 Experimentation and experience of materials and tools (eighteen months – eighteen years)

2 Symbolic interpretation (three – seven or eight years) based on holistic scanning and global vision, continuing into adult years as a valid option...

3 Predominantly symbolist approach (five – twelve years), there is evidence of a visual analytical approach...

4 Predominantly analytical approach from seven or eight years onwards: the need for visual realism is paramount but symbolist overtones will be apparent.

5 Analytical approach from eight or nine years onwards ... characterised by visual realism based on personal experience through the senses...

(Morgan, 1988)

Figure 10 *Mum and baby*, by girl aged four in charcoal

Symbolic representation is not an inferior way of drawing and although we encourage children by enabling them to look and see, we must not force children at nursery age into an analytic approach which is not appropriate to their age or experience. Indeed, some of the greatest artists in our century are great precisely because they have retained the power of drawing like a child, in a symbolic rather than an analytical way: see, for example, the work of Paul Klee.

The following story is an account of how the experience of drawing at her nursery school set a four-year-old girl free. The girl's teacher told us that this child did not do any drawing at all when she came to school. In fact she did not do much of anything, wandering around the nursery in a lost sort of way and hiding behind her mother when she arrived, giggling self-consciously. She seemed under-stimulated at home; it was, for example, hard to believe she'd ever done any drawing and was probably destined for special education of one kind or another.

Figure 11   *Nina and Dula,*
by girl aged four in charcoal

Eventually the girl drew because the materials to draw with were always there: pencils, wax crayons, biros, fine felt-tips, fat felt-tips, charcoal and paint and paper of various sizes and shades. All these things were always present in this nursery, because, as her teacher told us:

> They do all different things in their drawing. You might want something smudgy like charcoal or pastel, or you might want some close precision, so you'd use the biros...

Choice is vital as Robin Tanner said in an address to Wiltshire teachers, advisers and ex-pupils in 1984:

> ...choice demands rejection. Every creative act is an act of choosing ... we are all given this wonderful power ... to respect all kinds of material: human material, paper, cloth, wood, everything...

(Tanner, 1984)

This girl eventually drew, choosing pencil. This figure (figure 12) was probably the first mark she ever made on paper. Holding her pencil as you would hold a hammer, she scribbled and scratched; lightly, anxiously, spikily. She'd heard the other children telling the teacher what their drawings were, some in whole sentences: 'Here is my brother's bike', for example; and now she came out with her drawing, eyes down with their wide smiley look and said, 'Tiger'. Her teacher told us:

She doesn't string a sentence together at all, she doesn't say a word when her mother's there, she's like a kitten, like her drawings in fact...

Figure 12 *Tiger*, by girl aged four in pencil

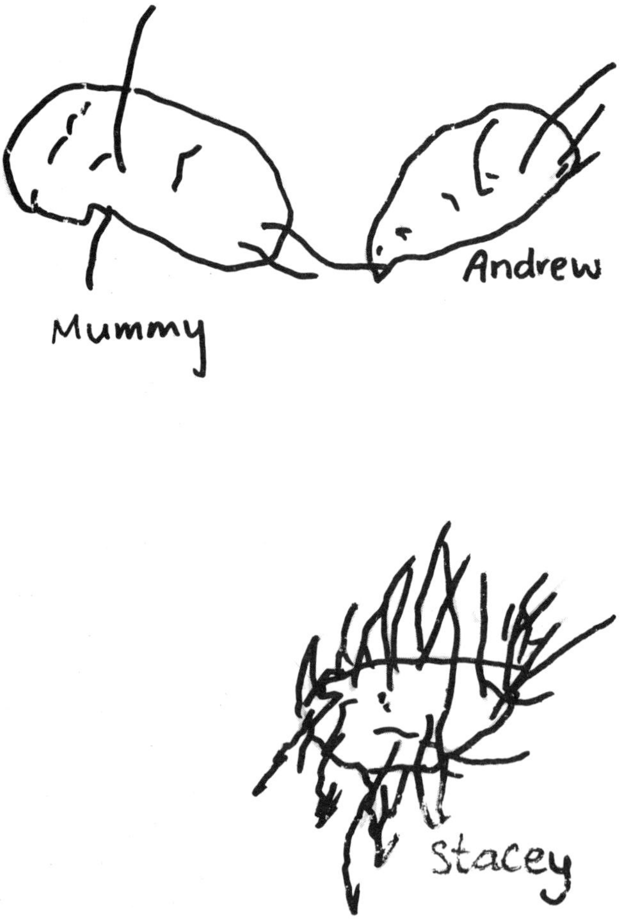

Figure 13 *Mummy, Andrew, Stacey*, by girl aged four in felt-tip

What normally happens to such drawings in a busy nursery? Sadly, too often, they are thrown in the bin at the end of the day. This one was marked by the nursery nurse with the child's name and that was just as well, because a week later the child drew the little figures in figure 13, *Mummy, Andrew, Stacey*.

Before we move on to discuss figure 13, consider for a moment the power of this child's first scribble seen in a learning context. Whenever a child does something for the first time, it looks cumbersome and awkward to an adult. Often, as with the tying of a shoelace, we are tempted to take over. But it is worth considering how strong the thrust of the learning process is in such a situation. The child who has never drawn is getting off the starting block and his/her work at this stage should be respected. It should be treated with the same involved attention as a child's first attempts at talking.

Indeed, there is an analogy here with talk. When a child struggles to express herself about, say, the way a brake on a bicycle works, the result may not be attractive to adult ears. She stumbles, breaks off, starts again, mumbles, mutters, frowns and puts her hand over her mouth. So all too often as adults we stop her and supply the answer. But it is in the struggle, the mutter, that the learning takes place. As with the first drawing, the mutterings, like the initial tentative lines, should be paid more respect than is often the case.

If we now take a close look at the figures in figure 13 we can see that they are recognisable representations of the rest of the child's family. How had this remarkable change in this girl's experience come about? The teacher told us:

> I planned for the children to paint with very long brushes. In fact, they were normal hoghair brushes, nine inches long, tied to rulers. I reckoned it would give them more scope, it would force them into a larger scale, it would set their muscles free to be a bit daring, it would involve what they call at college 'large motor skills' as well as small ones...As bad luck would have it, I couldn't be in the nursery the day they did the paintings, I had to go to a meeting somewhere else in the school, and there was a supply teacher in there...When I went back I thought the teacher had made a mistake, labelling these big drawings in black paint with the girl's name...[See figures

14 and 15 entitled 'Man'.] But they were hers.
I'd learnt something. The figures *had* been there in those
tight little squiggles, but I hadn't seen them. The eyes, the
nose, the mouth etc. were so tiny, or so obscured, so
confused, I'd not seen them ... I have learned now not to
be dismissive of what they do, to see it as an important
part of the learning process. This process is just as
important as what the adult can see as the final
product... The child had learned too, of course. After the
big brush work, the little figures were recognisable. She
restricted her number of lines. That stayed with her and
she will now draw bolder, stronger...

Figure 14   *Man,* by
girl aged four in black
paint

Figure 15   *Man,* by girl aged four in black paint

She was also learning the respect that Robin Tanner talked about: respect over her materials (human and inanimate) as she chose what to use and what to draw. She was also learning to take a pleasure, even a sensual delight, in the movement of her arm in its mark-making sweeps.

Later, near Christmas, the same teacher left all kinds of books around the room as well as reproductions including work by Picasso, various icons and photographs of a parent and a child. There was also an Indian mother and child and this encouragement to look at work from different cultural groups is something which we will continue to stress throughout this book.

The teacher asked one of the children to hold a doll in the middle of the room. This generated talk here about how you hold a baby: protecting the head and making sure the baby is comfortable. Then the children drew their own mother and child pictures. It is instructive to compare the drawings they made with the work that appears in many schools at Christmas time. Template stars and identical wise men made from the insides of toilet rolls, sets of angels decorated with silver spray: all this paraphernalia narrows the learning experience down to a sort of training. Templates take away from the child the power he/she might have over the shape of the image and their implicit message to the child is: what you can do is as nothing compared to this adult outline shape, this grown-up perception of what we are talking about. It is interesting to note that the work produced in such sessions bears no resemblance to works of fine art from our own or other cultures.

Template as a concept has a wider application than the literal one. It can also stand for the prescriptive ideas we have about life that we pass on to children, by failing to invite them to make decisions about anything. In art, for example, we sometimes convey the pre-eminence of the photograph as the image to be enjoyed, revered and imitated. In our displays we all too often implicitly teach children that the final product is all that matters. But the stages are crucial learning experiences and they need to be seen if we are to make sense of the culmination of our lessons. In fact our classrooms would be better off seen as workshops.

Figure 16 *Mother and child*, by girl aged four in pencil

Figure 18 *Mother and child*, by girl aged four in felt-tip

Figure 17 *Mother and child*, by boy aged four in charcoal

Figure 19 *Mother and child*, by boy aged four in charcoal, pencil and felt-tip

Figure 20   *Mother and child*, by girl aged four in charcoal

A child looked at a Picasso, using her charcoal with enormous vigour, never taking her eyes off the reproduction open on the table in front of her (see figure 20). If the National Curriculum is to emphasise learning about great artists, this is one very powerful way of encouraging that learning. But she learned other more important things, for example, something about what it is to be a mother holding a baby. She will have remembered some of her own experiences in her mother's arms and she will also have learned something about the materials that she used, the charcoal and paper. In other words, she and her friends are engaging emotionally, intellectually and physically with the world around them as they work in this way.

Figure 21   *Mother and child*, by girl aged four in felt-tip and charcoal

Another child talked as he drew figure 23 and his teacher wrote down what he said:

> The reindeer are asleep. Father Christmas is going to wake them up. One is smiling at him. One of its antlers is cracking. The daddy has got lots of horns. Father Christmas is going to give them all these buns to eat. The baby ones are eating all the buns. The buns have got all maggots in. The maggots are going all over the reindeers' faces. Father Christmas is going to get the maggots off because the reindeer are getting dead. The black man is looking at the reindeer. He has broken his fingers off with a hammer. The bee is going to sting him on his toes. The dragonfly is going to sting Father Christmas. My dad says they don't sting but my mum says they do. The one without a stinger is just going to fly off.

Figure 22 *Mother and child*, by girl aged four in charcoal

Figure 23 *The reindeers are asleep*, by boy aged four in felt-tip

This boy said all this as he drew. What is going on here? He is making-up a story. Too many of us assume that because children of this age can't write accurately, they can't make up stories. An artistic activity is leaving his mind free to roam over the sort of bizarre narrative that is familiar to those of us used to listening to children.

The story moves away from template Christmas sentimentality to horror. The boy is practising words he knows, to see if they are right in this context; a context which involves this piece of paper, this pencil, this woman called his teacher. And obviously, he is thinking.

His other drawings often display a distinctive style and a provisional coming to terms with his own anxieties, as for example, in his drawing *Mrs Sedgwick is crying because of a bad dream* (see figure 25). His mother and child study (figure 17) sees him solving a very difficult problem: the child is on the mother's knee and therefore hiding parts of the larger figure. Even much older children insist on the figures being separate. This exercise has set this boy a useful challenge.

It is worth remembering here something from *Art 7–11*:

> **. . . drawing is not so much a skill to be learnt as evidence produced of a thought process to use for learning. . .**

(Schools Council, 1978)

We define drawing here inclusively as mark-making: children draw with paint, print-making tools, scissors (as Matisse did towards the end of his life) as well as with the normal graphic tools. On one occasion we watched a child draw in three dimensions. However it works, drawing is thinking aloud, a powerful route into knowledge.

Figure 24 *Mrs Sedgwick and Lee*, by boy aged four in felt-tip

Figure 25 *Mrs Sedgwick is crying because of a bad dream*, by boy aged four in charcoal

2 Planning a scheme of work in mark-making

At one school which we visited a teacher gave us a scheme of work which she uses with pupils of eight-, nine-, and ten-years-of-age. We are reproducing this document here because it shows very clearly one way in which a developmental scheme might be designed. The graphic experiences are not left to chance but are carefully planned. Through such a course of lessons pupils learn in an organised way, some of the many ways of making marks to record impressions of the world they live in and their relationships to that world. The very fact that they have the opportunity to do this suggests to them that there are many other ways too, if only they were to go about discovering them. In other words such a scheme of work teaches a method for learning as well as teaching art.

This school struck us as one with a genuine commitment to learning through art. There was nothing merely ornamental about any of the work on display. The following scheme is an excellent example of a well-planned work scheme.

WORK SCHEME FOR YEAR FIVE: DRAWING AND MARK-MAKING

Aims:

1   to increase children's confidence in handling a variety of mark-making materials and equipment;

2   to increase children's ability to observe and record from a variety of natural and made resources;

3   to introduce the formal elements of tone, line, shape, form and texture as appropriate to the tasks being undertaken.

Tasks and materials		Stimulus
Stage one	pencil different marks tone, (light/dark) pencil portraits and/or observation of natural objects	other pupils
Stage two	chalk/charcoal qualities of line different marks observation	seed head/ natural objects
Stage three	pencil shapes, their relationships with other shapes	large still life
Stage four	mark-making fluid card, sponge, straws mark-making from observation introducing different textures	large still life
Stage five	torn paper as technique for recording (limited colour range) contrasts or torn and cut to achieve contrast of organic and artificial edges	large still life
Stage six	other materials could include pen, colour pens, felt-tips, ballpoints, brush and ink wash, chalks, pastels, crayon.	

Analysis of the drawing and mark-making work scheme

This scheme offers a variety of materials and methods for observing, remembering and imagining the world. The pupils are also exploring some of the elements of art and design. The components contained in this scheme are important for any sound basis in art education, especially taking into account present curriculum needs.

Of course, it is possible to make a scheme of work in any subject too programmatic. For instance, it is very rarely the case that children can only do certain things sequentially, that is, after they have done certain other things. Three five-year-olds illustrated Charles Causley's poem 'When I was a boy', which continues:

> On the Isle of Wight
> We all had a bath
> On Friday night . . .
>
> (Charles Causley, 1987)

They did this without any preparatory work except the normal drawing experiences which children get, if they are lucky. (See figure 26 below and figures C3 and C4 on page 98 in the colour section.)

Figure 26 *We all had a bath*, by girl aged five in pencil

Similarly, a seven-year-old drew this picture of his father's favourite jazz group while looking at a record cover and listening to the music: he did not draw the group accurately, of course, but he did draw with great feeling. No one will dispute the humour and frankness of these drawings, whether they meet any attainment targets or not.

Figure 27   *The Dave Brubeck Quartet, by boy aged eight in fine felt-tip*

We labour this point to show that children frequently make vivid art in happy, chance moments if there is a creative and supportive atmosphere in the classroom: a drawing corner, for example, and a wealth of materials and artefacts of various kinds, both originals and reproductions. Even more important than stimulating materials is the attitude of the adults, whether teachers, classroom helpers or parents. If the work is displayed so that children can relate, and even interact with it, so much the better. (See Margaret Jackson's book *Creative display and environment*, also in this series, for vivid examples of this.)

Nevertheless, some careful preparation can ensure that children gain a fuller experience of material and stimuli than is sometimes the case and the staff at this school have designed a scheme which is exemplary in its professionalism.

Mark-making work scheme stage one

Some teachers give children pieces of paper at the beginning of a drawing scheme and ask them to fill it with as many different pencil marks as possible. Even the very youngest school children, at four or five, can benefit from this exercise. Although it will only be a few minutes before some of them are bored (and therefore finished for the time being), others can concentrate for surprisingly long periods on this practical tool for researching different ways of mark-making.

However short the period, they will nevertheless discover that a pencil, charcoal or pastel, can do many more things than they had previously thought: scraping, smudging, almost cutting a fine line, cross-hatching, making soft marks with the side of the lead and numerous other forms of mark-making. The children explore the full range of pale to dark tones and enjoy the physical sensations involved in this intensive piece of learning. They are in fact exploring elements in art and design. This exercise is also useful for provoking children to talk about graphic tools and techniques.

Older children can spend over half an hour on this activity. It opens mental doors to many ways of making marks and at a stroke gives their drawings a greater variety and depth than they would previously have had. This fact can be demonstrated by looking at work by children who have had this experience and those who have not. It needs repeating again and again. Another version of this activity is to give children a sheet of A4 paper for example and to ask them to divide it into halves, then quarters, and finally sixteenths. They are then challenged to fill each rectangle with a different kind of pencil mark. In the present educational climate when everything we teach has to earn its time in the day, this exercise (like so much art), serves a double purpose, as it reinforces some of the language of mathematics. The nature of this experiment when it is tried in a constricted space is different in character from the open large paper-size approach. The latter often shows explosive, outward movements, while the former shows tighter, fitting shapes.

Let us now look at some work actually produced by a child following this work scheme. The sensitive drawing of a boy's head in figure 28 has a depth and emotional truthfulness about it which is not only the result of feeling but occurs when that feeling is combined with the techniques which the pupil has been shown in

Figure 28 *Alex*, by girl aged ten in pencil

the course of well-organised teaching. The artist has worked both practically and imaginatively to make a drawing which reveals strong feeling and which has incorporated a wide range of graphic techniques. It is encouraging that this girl has not been put off by her work's lack of photographic exactness and that she had produced a drawing of emotional honesty.

Mark-making work scheme stage two

Stage two of this scheme involved chalk and charcoal. These tools suggest to children that exact images are not the only kind: that there are more ways of drawing than are dreamed of in a philosophy bounded (and restricted) by cartoon characters and the influence of the camera in magazines and advertisements. The introduction of drawings and reproductions which show the expressive qualities of this kind of work should play a part at this stage.

The apparently scruffy, dirty line produced by chalk or charcoal has a presence and power lacked by a pencil line. It also teaches something in its less erasable quality. When we look at Giacometti's drawings we are aware of one of two facts, depending on our temperament: there is no such thing as a wrong line; or, wrong lines are valuable in giving a drawing vigour. Drawings that have alternative lines left in (that suggest several options have been pursued), teach us that nothing is objective. From what point of view do we look at things? On that, of course, depends the images we present and an image that offers different options has the virtue of existential honesty. Chalk and charcoal have parts to play in this aspect of art that the more tentative pencil lacks.

Although the teazel is something of a cliché in many schools as a subject for close observational drawing, it is still a powerful image (see figure 29). This is the kind of work which so thoroughly engages the mind and the senses that a hush falls on a group of children engaged in it. It calms them. It seems hard to misbehave as you draw, much as it is hard to misbehave as you make music. (See also the still life drawings in figures C5–C10(a) and (b) on pages 99–102 in the colour section.)

Figure 29 *Teazle*, by girl aged ten in chalk and charcoal

Why we draw is an issue addressed by Henry Moore:

Drawing is a means of finding your way about things, and a way of experiencing more quickly, certain tryouts and attempts.

(Newland and Rubens, 1984)

In other words, drawing is not a question of *recording* learning ('You've seen HMS *Victory*, a dead pigeon, this teazel: now draw them') but a *process* of learning. Much as we learn by writing or dancing or by playing an instrument, so we learn as we draw.

Close observational drawing plays a major role in art education and each drawing must be seen as one in a series of stages, not as an isolated, single end-product. We as teachers can learn so much about children and the way they are thinking, developing and meeting problems, when we watch them draw.

Figure 30   *Alligator*, by girl aged eight in charcoal

The children who produced these drawings were learning: not only about the nature of the object they were presented with, or about the tools they were using to learn, but also about their relationship with that object. In another school, a child has looked at a South American balsa-wood alligator in the same engaged way and created a charcoal drawing (see figure 30 above). In yet another school, a six-year-old has learned about his 'nanna'. This example is especially interesting because he has been offered the opportunity to learn about her in two ways: he has written as well as drawn. As we mentioned earlier, far too often drawing and writing are separated but why do we so often deny children one of these learning opportunities (usually, it must be said, to the detriment of drawing) when the opportunity is there to give children a choice? This boy has used his pencil in many ways (see figure 31), but he has also written:

Figure 31   *My Nanna*,
by boy aged six in pencil

my nannas Hair is white and CURLY. mine is brown and tangley. My nannas skin is crinkley and bumpy and her eyes are blue and crinkles on her neck.

Newland and Rubens (1984) also point out that:

> Children who learn to look, learn to question, to discover and to understand. Looking through drawing prolongs the looking...

Mark-making work scheme stage three

Stage three in the scheme was the still life drawing. Still lives in themselves can be wonderful tools for challenge or, alternatively, very boring. They require thought in regard to the shapes of the components offered and the spaces between those components. The background is as important as the objects.

Figure 32 *Still life*, by girl aged ten in charcoal

Figure 34 *Still life*, by girl aged ten in felt-tip

Figure 35 *Still life*, by boy aged ten in pencil

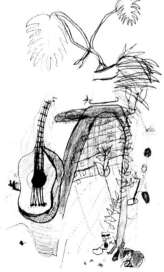

Figure 33 *Still life*, by girl aged ten in pencil

Notice how the pencil, charcoal and felt-tips have been used in figures 32–36: the side of the pencil lead scraping, the heavy dark lines, the light frail lines, the careful smudging, the cross-hatching. There is: roughness and gentleness, light and shade, thickness and thinness and all these contrasts have been learnt in the process of completing the previous, less finished work, so that the cumulative effect of these experiences is to deepen the intensity of these drawings.

Figure 36 *Still life*, by girl aged ten in pen and ink

Mark-making work scheme stage four

The children then went on to make marks with more unusual tools: sponges, torn edges of card, their fingers. One teacher said:

> They learn here that they could make marks with their toes if it seemed appropriate.

This work is less common in schools, perhaps because it has a less finished look about it. It is a product less likely to impress the indiscriminate visiting governor, who, perhaps, judges art on its photographic qualities, rather than on its experimental ones. It has, however, a value as a process of learning; it teaches the artist to widen the range of his/her techniques and to explore the elements of art and design at first hand. This variety was also apparent in another school where a ten-year-old girl drew with a knife on a scraper board to produce *Sheep's skull* (figure 37) and another child made her marks with weaving. (See figure C11 on page 103 in the colour section.)

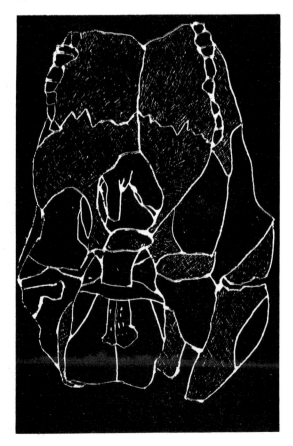

Figure 37 *Sheep's skull*, by girl aged ten in scraper board

Mark-making work scheme stage five

Finally the children developed the still life, re-working it in terms of collage: torn and cut paper. Some teachers show children examples of what Matisse did in this area. When he could no longer hold a brush, he drew with scissors, beginning with his famous images of the monstera plants and moving on to simple and very telling images of women and the work he did for the book *Jazz*. Children need to be encouraged to make rough lines by tearing the paper as well as cutting it. These pupils could also have reconstructed their still lives in terms of collages in other materials: paper from magazines, hessian and other bits and pieces from the scrap box. (See figures C12 and C13 on pages 104–5 in the colour section.)

Mark-making work scheme stage six

These children had been exposed to an impressive variety of materials and methods as the work scheme recommended at stage six, and it was this variety and intensity of experience that had matured the pupils' work so soundly.

CONCLUSION

The children involved in this teacher's work scheme had learned that each subject, especially the still life, had a number of qualities and that each of these qualities could be focused on and brought out. They had arrived at a point where they could make pen and ink drawings of the same still life arrangement that they had drawn earlier, which verged on the abstract. These drawings demonstrate that the abstract is not a breaking off, or an anarchic freedom from, the constraints of good drawing, but an organic growth which occurs when we work in the rich variety of ways which the National Curriculum refers to constantly in phrases like 'experiment and apply knowledge'.

The studies of nuts and swedes in figures C14 and C15 on pages 107–8 in the colour section are the climax of this kind of work. The pupils have explored their subjects with an emotional intensity which is not spoilt by technical expertise but enhanced by it. This may seem to be an obvious point to make but all too often in the arts there is the impression that feelings are contaminated when, for example, we 'tear apart' a poem. All art is a meeting between technique and feeling. Indeed, it is arguable that the greater the concentration on technique, the greater the opportunity the feeling has to be truly expressed in a way which communicates its meaning to others. However, there are often, of course, delightful results produced by those lacking technique; in the purely spontaneous and inspirational. The tortoise in figure 38 was drawn by a boy in a unit for language impaired children. He was watching the teacher's pet tortoise eating a banana.

Figure 38 *Tortoise, by boy aged six in pencil*

Finally, remember not to make a work scheme too programmatic. Surprise them, give the children a jolt with the unexpected. The different is nearly always educational. For instance one teacher we visited had a childlike quality: she collected. When we visited her school, she had in her classroom a neat hoard of hubcaps. She put them around the room for an art lesson and provided soft crayons. The children simply travelled round the room choosing images from the circles of metal to rub on to their paper. (See figures 39 and 40.) Again, the vigour of the results, together with the ease with which they were achieved, is educational in several ways. It offered a visual vigour to children who believed that they were less gifted in a preconceived traditional approach to art. It provides children with yet another example from the variety of art contained in the great human store. It provides a talking point about printing and it shows that it is not only grand images that provide art but homely ones too, like a motor firm's logo, or a perfect circle from the rim of a discarded hubcap. This experience, by its very nature, must include thought, selection, rejection, experimentation, experience of the elements of art and design, and personal evaluation.

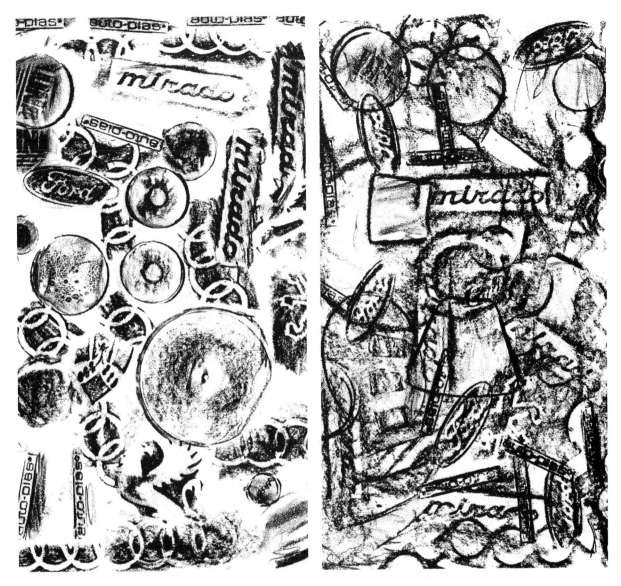

Figure 39 *Hub-cap rubbing*, by boy aged nine in black wax crayon

Figure 40 *Hub-cap rubbing*, by girl aged nine in black wax crayon

It is as well that we give children jolts like this from time to time, whether in terms of the materials we offer them, or in the subject matter provided, because it helps them to understand the wider definitions of the art of drawing. It helps them to experiment and to apply knowledge gained in other experiences and it pushes their explorations of the elements of art and design beyond predictable boundaries. That in itself can only be educational.

3 Some aspects of drawing from direct experience

Most good schools have encouraged children to work from direct experience and have displays of artefacts and objects of many different kinds. Although this kind of close observational work can be something of a cliché, it is undoubtedly still a powerful way of learning. The triangle formed by the lines between eye, hand and the subject is intensely educational. This still applies, of course, when we are studying natural objects: plants in a pot or waves breaking on the shore for example.

CHOOSING A SUBJECT WHICH INSPIRES NEW WAYS OF SEEING

The first thing the teacher must do is find interesting things for the children to work from. The time has passed when a group of dull and apparently unrelated items constituted the challenge presented to children for their drawing lesson. But what is interesting to children? It is less the nature of the object itself which is interesting than the way that they are encouraged to look at it. Perhaps there is no such thing as a dull item if it is introduced by a teacher who has the ability to inspire children to do some real seeing.

Professional artists always have a reason for drawing, although they may well not translate it into words. The designer has a brief but the fine artist moves among a variety of possibilities, driven by his/her own interests and responses to the world, for example, the overall pattern, the shape, the character, the mood, the story, the message.

Some children feel their own way towards their personal statement but even these independent youngsters can be more intensely involved and stimulated by good presentation on the part of the teacher. One way to achieve an intensity in one's work is to look with new eyes at the item or items, either in isolation, or in their particular setting and to channel the children's energies into particular aspects of the subject matter. This can be achieve by focusing their attention on particular aspects of the subject doing, encouraging new ways of seeing.

Example challenges

- Look at the different shapes which you can see in the reflection in the tin, or spoon, or crumpled foil.
- Look at the shapes which you can see in the guinea pig and the texture and pattern of its fur.
- Look at the shapes and patterns in the pylon which we can see from the window.
- Look at the darks and lights which we can see in that little group of items placed in a big, deep box lying on its side and lit by a bicycle lamp or torch.
- Look at the pattern on that part of the shell.
- Look at the shapes in that collection from a garage: cogs, gaskets, bits of piping and tubing.
- Look at my car engine while it is quiet and now as I turn the ignition on.

Each one of these challenges links an element of art to a way of seeing a subject. It is a question of the teacher seeing and triggering the children to do the same.

However young the child, this approach is valid. But it is important to be open to responses from young children which seem to have little to do with the subject matter, or which are, at least in part, of a symbolic order rather than an analytic one. (See chapter one for a further discussion of this.) Even analytic work has overtones of the expressive: we are not robots or cameras, but feeling beings. Similarly, there are strong links between expressive drawing and other disciplines which are analytical in nature, such as science and engineering.

It is always useful for schools to build up collections of items, together with resource knowledge of where to get such things. Helpful caretakers are always useful, as they have cleaners, buffers and other tools in store which make for interesting drawings. Years ago, in a primary school where one of us worked, the heating frequently broke down. This was a cause of irritation and sometimes distress but the butane heaters (the children called them daleks), were, on one occasion, exciting visual objects for the children to draw.

The underlying principle behind this work is that everything is visually interesting if we look hard enough, and that there are many ways of learning about it. George Herbert wrote:

**Who sweeps a room, as for God's law,
Makes that and the action fine...**

(George Herbert (1593–1633), 1961)

By a similar token, anyone who looks at the ordinary objects of our lives through the eyes of a learning artist and with a mind open to the myriad ways of making marks can make those objects fine too.

Look at the fire extinguisher on the wall for example; or the broken telephone that a father who works for British Telecom has given the school; the out-of-date computer printer; the broken lawnmower. The disgusting pile of PE slippers is an eyesore until we transform it through art, by careful observation and drawing.

Get the children to take the mechanical things apart and look for shapes in them. As they are doing this, they are learning science and maths and design and technology. They are, for example, recognising important similarities and differences in the characteristics of materials, including hardness, flexibility and transparency as well as recognising geometrical shapes. They are, however, also observing, remembering and imagining: using practical things and working mentally to turn them into art forms.

PROVIDING THE RIGHT GRAPHIC TOOLS

Once we have found exciting items for children to examine, we must make sure that the children have the chance to experience different kinds of graphic tool. This means stretching the potential of the instruments to the extreme and giving the children sufficient time and motivation to see what they do. They need ballpoints, felt-tip pens, pencils, crayons, charcoal, chalk: each of these tools has a lesson to teach children. If we see the tools themselves as teachers we immediately open ourselves up to a world of possibilities. By asking ourselves the question: what else is available for children to make marks with in drawing? We can extend the range of available tools immeasurably. They can try whatever can be found, from scraps of cardboard perhaps, to bits of wood.

ACTIVE LEARNING THROUGH DRAWING AND WRITING
FROM DIRECT EXPERIENCE

It was a headteacher (one of those who still considers himself a member of the teaching profession, as well as a manager of it) who told us the following story. Although this headteacher taught drawing and painting most days he was still disconcerted to hear at eight-thirty one morning that his reception teacher would be in late because of a break-in at her house. He told us:

I was anxious to find something for the children to do that would be relevant, to say the least, to the National Curriculum and still true to my principles of treating children as active learners and using firsthand experiences wherever possible. So, in other words, helping children to learn through play, not just instruction. As I walked worriedly through the school, I saw the nursery teacher and the nursery nurse getting their classroom ready and on the spur of the moment I asked them if I could borrow one of the bicycles that the children use there.

Later I set the bicycle upside down on a small table and spun the front wheel and asked the five-year-olds to listen. We were sitting on the carpet around the bike and all of us stared up at it. What were they thinking? What's that there for? What's he up to now? What are we going to do?

I whizzed the wheel round. 'What does that sound like?' I asked, thinking it sounded like the cicadas around the hotel in Sorrento last summer, drowning the olive groves with their bicycle noises. Then, coming back down to earth, I pulled the brake handle. 'How did that happen? Why did that stop?'

I have to say that *I* was learning here! I have played with wheels and brakes sometimes, often to very little purpose. I knew the wheel would turn faster than the pedals, with one part of my brain. But this experience was very vivid, very engaging, very interesting and I was learning more and more. I learnt more about the power of gears on the chain and cog arrangement. Indeed, I went on learning throughout the following hour, as I talked to the children and played with the bike.

But if I was learning, what was happening in those attentive, immature minds? Four-year-old Gemma watched intently. 'That tube ... there's something in it ... it made that black thing go on the wheel.'

The class watched as the chain turned slowly and the wheels turned fast. They discussed how that was happening. Part of their brains knew already too, part didn't. This was a way in which we were linked. I asked about the handlebars: 'What does the shape of these remind you of?' and about the smell of the bike and what parts of it felt like.

That evening I found the following in *Science in the National Curriculum* at various levels that the children had begun to hit, or reach, or cover, I'm not sure of the target metaphor:

- Pupils should observe familiar materials and events in their immediate environment, at firsthand, using their senses.
- Pupils should describe and communicate their observations, ideally through talking in groups or by other means, within their class.
- Pupils should be able to describe familiar and unfamiliar objects in terms of simple properties, for example, shape, colour, texture...
- Pupils should know that things can be moved by pushing them and (Level 2) understand that pushes and pulls can make things start moving, speed up, swerve or stop.

In English, the children were hitting, if not reaching, Attainment Target 1, *Speaking and Listening*, which says that pupils should 'participate as speakers and listeners in group activities'. But in art and design the children were gaining even more. They were thinking, observing, remembering, imagining: as they began their drawings they were using a variety of materials and methods.

Following a similar lesson a six-year-old in a unit for children with language difficulties drew her bicycle with extraordinary vigour (see figure 41). The speech therapist working with these children told us how important it was that children with these sorts of difficulties should have a chance to excel at art:

> All too often they have to concentrate on what are called the basics, while they can succeed in this kind of work.

Figure 41 *Bicycle*, by girl aged six in pencil

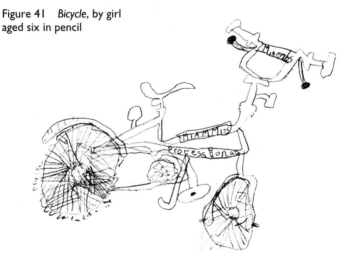

Art offers success to many children and therefore builds their confidence up for other areas of learning, as well as being a valid mode of learning in its own right.

Of course, you can also use bicycles in more familiar modes: being ridden down a hill, for example, or even being crashed. Some more colourful tools will help children to draw bicycles in a less realistic, more expressive mode and enhance a different quality in analytic investigation. (See figures C16–18 on page 109 in the colour section.)

In the following poem, the bike is at first being mended. The writer feels that when it's upside down it looks like a pair of old-fashioned glasses, later turned the right way up, it resembles an animal with a pair of antlers.

Kelly Jane's Bike

A pair of wire-framed spectacles. Antlers
   on a skinny creature
upside down, at rest, ticking over till
   you pull the brake-wire through
its tube to stop the blurred rapid patter.

   An oily mess of chain
that prints roughly on your hands. Laid up in
   the shed, the bike is
waiting, one tyre holed and useless till he
   baptises, finds the flaw,

and sends you ('Go carefully Kelly now')
   to Seva's shop for milk.
You hiss down the rainy hill, a goddess
   clutching antlers again,
proud over short-sighted ladies, and dogs,
   and small children walking.

(Fred Sedgwick, to be published 1994)

A nine-year-old wrote this poem on being asked to remember and reflect on a bike ride:

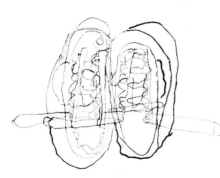

Stop wind!
Stop being greedy by taking my bike
as you do with the leaves
and the puddles that lay peacefully
on the floor
until you came along.
The wind is blowing me back.
My bike jolts like an old car.
I'm turning, I'm skidding, I'm wobbling.
BANG! The wind has won.

Figure 42 *Section of bicycle*, by boy aged nine in pencil

The teacher had asked her a series of questions like those below to help her direct and focus her attention.

Example questions

- What is the wind like? Can you say something about this with an adjective, a describing word?
- What is the movement of your bike like? Can you put it in a verb, a doing word?
- Can you make me feel as if *I'm* on your bike in the wind?
- Can you make sure you use words that the others won't think of?

As with most children's drawing and writing, the key is firsthand experience. The children are not drawing or writing about *bikes* but about a particular bike. Put it upside down on the table. Placing it this way up makes it unfamiliar and making the ordinary extraordinary, or the familiar unfamiliar, or the every day strange is a useful way of making children look. At this point in their education, the critical need is to get the children to talk: not to tell them things, but to get them to explain to each other their understandings. The following list outlines some approaches which we considered using with the children.

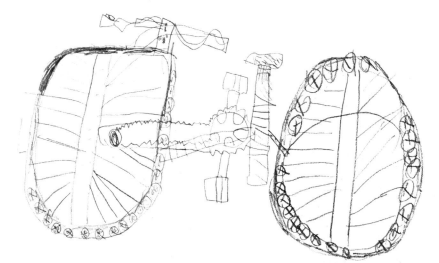

Figure 43 *Bicycle*, by boy aged nine in pencil

Example approaches

- Listen to this noise (you spin the wheel). Give me some words to describe it. Give me some words which sound like it. Look hard at the wheel as it turns, first slowly ... and then faster. What makes it stop? Suppose you drew the wheel doing those things.

- Look what happens now (you apply the brake). How did that happen? (Get them to reason it right through: the handle, the wire, the tubing, the block.) Don't foreclose the learning by telling them things. This reasoning is essential for the scientific, technological, linguistic and artistic learning which is going on.

- Look at these (show them the handlebars). What do they remind you of? The shape? The colour? Look how the light shines here and not here.

- Look at the wheel. What can you see? What materials are there here? What are these (the spokes) for?

- Can you smell the bike?

- What do the different parts of it feel like?

- Look at the spokes. What do you think they are for?

- Look at the lamp.

- Look at someone sitting on the bike.

If you can get more than one bike into the classroom, it is obviously advantageous, because the children can then get that much closer to their subject. The whole area of design and technology can be introduced with this topic. Get them to examine the bike closely, so that they can begin to work out how the chain and the pedals relate to the wheels. Ask them how the bike works, they can then reinforce this learning and take it further, through careful drawing.

We often tell children that they might draw only part of the bike. (See figures 42, 44, 45 and 46.) But whatever they do, they are challenged to draw what they are looking at close-up, so that we can see details. We make it clear that we accept wrong lines: 'Leave them there, just do the right line as well!' and we go so far as to remove erasers because they reinforce so strongly the post-photographic neurosis about exactness.

Figure 44 *Section of bicycle*, by boy aged nine in pencil

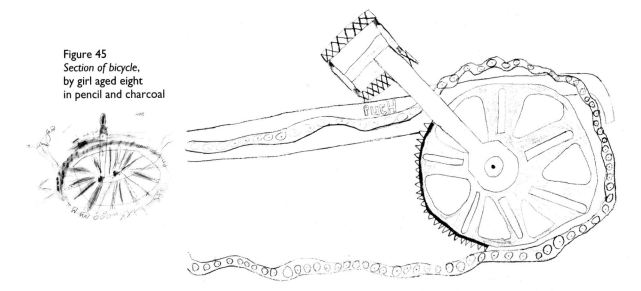

Figure 45
Section of bicycle,
by girl aged eight
in pencil and charcoal

Figure 46   *Section of bicycle*, by boy aged nine in pencil

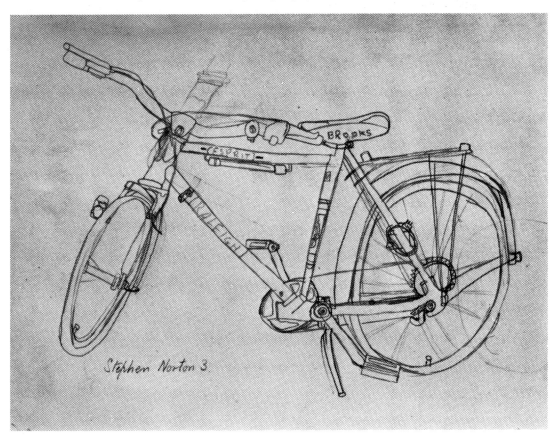

Figure 47   *Bicycle*, by boy aged eleven in pencil

Another powerful firsthand experience which can contribute greatly to children's learning in English, science and technology is the engine of your car. Take them out to the car park in small groups and let them look and listen hard and then start your car up. The following extracts are from writing done by ten-year-old children based on this experience with an engine. The teacher asked them to look for comparisons between the objects they were looking at and objects and living things from other areas of their experiences. He asked them to think about verbs that have a presence and a power, for example: shudder; crash; sprinting.

> I can feel the sharp blades of the fan, the spark plugs all ready to ring out, the pistons ready to crash into action. The key turns and the engine shudders, the fan sprinting around, the battery firing the spark plugs... The pistons shudder power into the grating gearbox as fumes choke themselves out of the exhaust... The wide black air cooler is like a squashed tin, trying to cool the engine working itself into hysterics.

> Our engine is getting louder as it purrs past a smelly, fumy lorry. Now it's speeding over the road ahead.

> The friction mounts in me,
> shock absorbers fly out of me
> as well as a lot of other shaped springs.
> A high-pitched whine comes from me.
> The force is channelled through someone's leg
> while the arms move like pistons
> through a never-ending pattern of a triangle.
> Other arms fly back and forth like a coupling rod.

The connection with art here is that the children drew far more vividly after this writing because the writing had made them look more closely. Writing and drawing frequently feed each other and we lose an opportunity to reinforce the learning potential of both if they are divorced in the classroom.

A child will hypothesise: 'I think that is for...' as she stares into the engine. It takes little imagination for us to consider how we might push the child on to further investigations on the strength of this hypothesis. If this seems like odd material for a book on children drawing to learn, we might reflect on the fact that the way we learn is not circumscribed by artificial subject barriers. Nature did not design the world in terms of science, technology, art and language. The world is there for both children and teachers to learn about and learning is what we want to happen, what *must* happen if we are to be professionals. Who cares, in the end, whether it happens through language or art?

The following are examples of questions which will help children to draw an engine, or part of it.

Example questions

- What materials is this made from?
- How do you think it was made?
- What do you think that part is for?
- What does that part feel like?
- What does the shape of that part remind you of?

Figure 48   *Church*

If you think that this is art dirtying its fingers in the world of science and technology, you would be right. In fact, the creative artist was at work before these things were made. Without him/her they would not exist and there must have been many trials and errors, many experiments and modifications on the way to the final product.

The bike and the engine are, of course, just two of many ideas for close observation work. Churches and graveyards, houses and other buildings (or parts of them), are also interesting and productive subjects for drawing from direct experience, as are places of purchase and commerce such as shops and supermarkets. Classroom-based projects can be based on objects as common-place and utilitarian as the shoe, the idea being to make children look again at the ordinary and to really see. The drawings in figures 48–52 illustrate just how effective drawing from direct experience can be.

Figure 49   *Church*

54

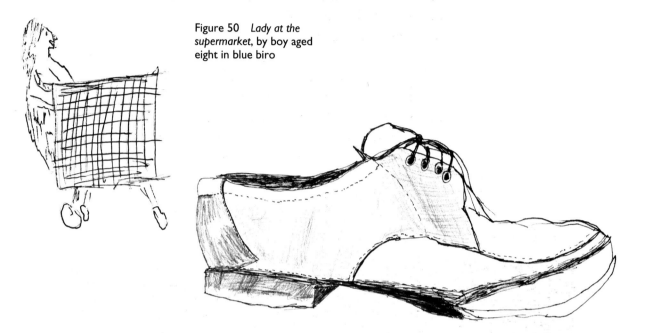

Figure 50 *Lady at the supermarket*, by boy aged eight in blue biro

Figure 51 *Shoe*, by boy aged ten in pencil and black biro

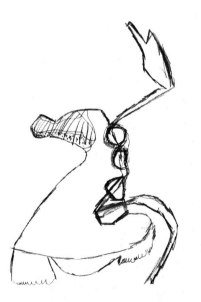

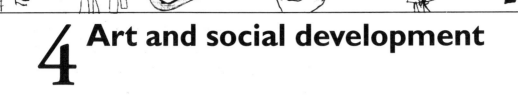

4 Art and social development

ART, SCHOOL AND THE WHOLE CHILD

We all understand that schools are not just about the subjects taught, but about the development of the child's whole life. The hidden curriculum, which we take so much for granted, is based on an understanding of the holistic nature of every human being and if our relationships with others are awry, our education is impaired. This has important implications for the teaching of art. After all, what set of subjects has more to say about our emotional and social lives than the arts? The following examples illustrate how art in schools plays a central role in the social development of our children.

A child in a nursery experienced the trauma of having his baby brother die. How should a school deal with this situation? We don't mean, of course, how should a school sort it out, because no one could do that but the arts are about materials, feelings and communication and therefore art can be the medium through which we come to terms with the appalling confusion that constitutes bereavement.

The child drew a distressed mother (see figure 53, *Mummy is crying*). There was no way to deal with this, other than to have an atmosphere in the school which allowed the child to express himself when life was difficult. Such an environment, in which the child is confident enough to externalise the traumas which have occurred and to have them accepted, helps the healing process.

Our second example concerns two teachers who were working on the sex education part of their Personal and Social Education (PSE) syllabus. The children they were working with were a group of ten- and eleven-year-olds who frequently presented behaviour problems. The school they attended is well-known for (amongst other things) the feeling the children generate through their drawings and the techniques they are taught: not through specifically technical lessons but through having the materials constantly available and having innovative work praised and encouraged. It is a listening school, where children's oral, written and artistic contributions are respected.

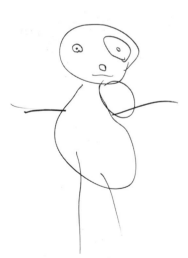

Figure 53 *Mummy is crying*, by boy aged four in black felt-tip and biro

In other words, the children explore the elements of art and design by constantly having a wide variety of materials and methods around them. This becomes very apparent when we see the quality of the work they produce. One of the teachers working on the sex education syllabus said about their project:

We used a mishmash of materials to get it going, photographs from magazines, family snapshots, stuff supplied by the multicultural centre. James's drawing [figure 55] is interesting to me in several ways: it was done from a photograph of one of my children ... I was holding her and you can just see my thumb on her waist. James's took a small part of the picture and enlarged it.

Figure 54 *Baby*, by boy aged nine in pencil

Figure 55 *Baby*, by boy aged ten in pencil

It's a virtuoso piece of drawing. He's very competent. I don't know how much feeling there is in it, it seems to be about solving problems of space. It's a larger piece of paper than we usually offer children working with pencil, about 60cm × 40cm... It's also quite academic for a drawing from this school, but I suppose babies aren't necessarily that interesting to eight-year-olds, especially some boys! .. Look how he's letraseted his name strongly, he's proud of this piece, that's significant...

(The child's name does not appear in the reproduction shown in this text.)

James's attempts at light and shade (where the hands tuck under the chin, under the elbow on the left and on the underside of the forearms) are not the result of any overt technical teaching but rather result from challenges to look and the constant availability of encouragement and materials. No one has ever said 'You can do cross hatching like this, or use the side of the lead like this' but all these techniques have been used and were constantly visible to this child ever since he started school five years before producing this drawing. The eyes look to one side and despite what the teacher says about it being academic it is a moving drawing because of the fœtal position of the baby. However, what moved us most were the capital letters printed at the bottom of the paper (deleted from our reproduction) which showed how pleased and proud the boy was of his work.

Sometimes teachers discourage this kind of marking – this statement that, like Kilroy, 'I was here, I exist', because it spoils the final effect. Yet sometimes there is a case for letting children mark their work in this way. James was a boy with problems, constantly in competition with his friends and, one suspects, with the adults who came and went in his home. He had little social success, so that when there was an occasion when he was a success (such as with this picture) he celebrated it in his own way.

The teacher told us that:

> We made a big thing about hands for this work. Being held, what it meant and so on ... my colleague said, don't bother with features if they're that much of a problem ... get the hands right ... look at your hands as they hold things ... look at my hands as they grip, as they punch, as they pick something up, as they stroke...

As a result of this direction the pictures concentrate on the hands, to the extent that one of them (figure 58) doesn't even have a face. (See figure C19 on page 110 in the colour section for more work of this nature.)

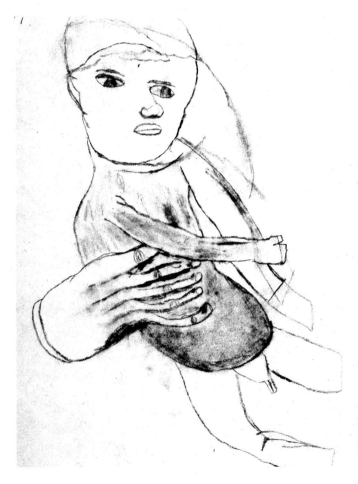

Figure 56 *Baby*, by girl aged ten in charcoal

Figure 58 *Baby,*
by boy aged ten in
pencil

Figure 57 *Baby,*
by boy aged nine in
charcoal and chalk

This kind of work is particularly important for children who have difficulties expressing their feelings without resorting to violence. The tenderness in these drawings is at odds with much of their playground behaviour and one hopes that some of the tenderness brought out by their art will spill over into the playground.

The stimuli which produced this work were very varied. Not only was there the 'mishmash of materials' that the teacher mentioned but also photographs from magazines and snap-shots from family albums. The children had also seen a mother with a baby in school, with the mother bathing and feeding her daughter. One of the teachers had also brought in a selection of photographs of himself with his daughter and was able to talk freely and unselfconsciously about the birth and upbringing of his children. The children had also experienced other more conventional elements of sex education, such as schools' television programmes.

The results were equally as varied as the stimuli which inspired the work. Whereas some of the children produced the large pictures shown in figures 56–58 other children used a great deal of space to make simple, relatively small images. The obvious question and one that as teachers we so often ask is: 'What about all this space, why don't you use all this up?' It may be true in some cases that tiny work in a sea of space is a result of a lack of confidence but it would be simplistic to interpret this as the only reason.

Although children do sometimes need encouragement to make the most of all their materials, including paper, there are other times when the white space is eloquent and necessary and we should neither encourage them to fill it, nor trim it off. One child, when asked if he thought there was too much space round his tiny, careful drawing, considered the question for what seemed to the teacher to be a long time and then replied: 'No, it's just right.' What courage this answer must have taken in the face of the perceived power of the teacher!

CREATING AN ENVIRONMENT FOR SOCIAL AND ACADEMIC DEVELOPMENT THROUGH ART

Successful work of this quality which enables children to observe, remember and imagine and which uses a variety of materials won't just happen. Likewise it won't take root in a classroom where the teacher is the only one in the school with these interests. In other words the school which wants to help children communicate, express and learn in a visual form, has to have a whole school policy. There has to be a sort of micro-tradition, so that seven-year-olds remember drawing experiences from their nursery days and eleven-year-olds remember similar experiences from when they were seven. They can then build up their aesthetic experiences both in terms of making their own art and design and in responding to that of others.

There has to be an atmosphere in the school which encourages looking, listening and personal experimentation and which works against the tyranny of the photographic image. This image leads to frenetic erasing of 'wrong' lines and the tracing of cartoon characters because the child has no confidence in his/her own statements. Problems arise for teachers in schools where there is no management backing for a policy on art, or drawing in particular. Sometimes this means that the headteacher isn't interested in this area of the curriculum but sometimes it simply means that he/she is so hard pressed that there isn't time for it because of the insistent demands of the core disciplines within the curriculum.

Teachers concerned with drawing have to make a sure defence of their subject in terms of the National Curriculum. There is now a stated need:

- to record observations from direct experience;
- to respond to memory and imagination;
- to explore a range of tools, materials and techniques;
- to talk about children's own work;
- to look at and talk about examples of work by well-known artists from a variety of periods and cultures.

All of this has been made very explicit in the National Curriculum for England and Wales but how do you implement it in a school without a policy on art? It is worth building up a schedule of attainment targets from different subject curriculum documents and demonstrating how drawing can enrich the children's experience in these areas. For example, where the National Curriculum for science says that pupils should:

observe familiar materials and events in their immediate environment, at firsthand, using their senses . . .

we can point out (and more importantly, demonstrate) how much more powerful this observation will be if they draw as they observe.

Likewise, if children are to:

understand how living things are looked after [and] be able to recognise similarities and differences both within and between different groups of plants and animals . . .

(National Curriculum, *Science*)

they need the kind of intense, concentrated, engaged looking that only accompanies drawing. Other examples can be found in different curriculum areas.

The practice of drawing is a crucial requirement for every child, and a developmental programme in class is a basic necessity. But the strategy of forming a drawing club beyond this class-work and displaying the children's work in assemblies and on walls will help to develop drawing within a school. (See Margaret Jackson's book, *Creative display and environment* (1993) in this series for clear guidelines on displays which are more than mere window-dressing.) Display can be used as educational material for teachers and children. It can suggest that art is more than a peripheral activity and that it has a central place in our learning, whether we are children or adults.

Another way of creating a whole school policy is to write a plan of work in a particular area of art, like the one in chapter two. When this is written by a group of two or three enthusiasts in a school, it soon has an impact beyond those who produced it as other members of staff appreciate the vigour of the work which begins to emerge.

ART IN THE CURRICULUM: A CENTRAL ELEMENT

What should the relationship between art and the rest of curriculum be? It is imperative that integrating art into all areas of the curriculum doesn't result in a watering-down of art into something purely decorative rather than a subject of central importance. Fred Sedgwick wrote in *The Expressive Arts* (Fulton, 1993) how the visual arts can become little more than slaves where they are used, for example, for painting stage scenery in an unimaginative way, or for illustrating a new historical topic. 'Let's have twenty Viking shields' the teacher might say, 'And let's make sure they are all perfect circles...' This kind of work destroys art and design's necessary autonomy, it relegates it to a purely illustrative, rather than emotionally expressive role and can teach children that it has a low status in the curriculum: what we do with the subject matter is arguably more important than what we actually teach.

However this is not to say that art exists in a vacuum (for its own sake) as though it didn't by its very nature feed off life and, just as importantly, nourish it. Indeed, art can have a part to play in the Viking topic, or any other element of the curriculum which we might choose to use as an example but it must be used positively, integrally, and not merely as an afterthought. We might take children to a museum to look at shields and we might ask questions such as those shown on the next page.

Example questions

- What are they for?
- How do they work?
- What are they made of?
- Why are the shields arranged as they are?
- Are they perfect circles?
- How could your drawing show what this material is?
- What can we do to record the texture and the way the light plays?

This kind of work clearly helps to develop children's drawings but it also helps them to learn history by encouraging them to think about what life was like for their antecedents. Of course it could also lead to drama. Similarly it can help them to learn about their personalities and their social relations by helping them to work collaboratively.

However, art is a central element in personal and social education (PSE) in more explicit ways than those mentioned above as it helps children to come to terms, albeit provisionally, with their world and their relationship to it. While we need explicit teaching of PSE, art and design, with their emphasis on the celebration of our essential humanity, offer much to this area; so much in fact that we neglect it at the children's peril.

The face in figure 59 is by a boy of four who is profoundly deaf. It seems to us that it can be a mistake to build a huge apparatus of interpretation around children's drawings, using psychological terms. This is because it can sell art short and make it a slave again: this time to behaviourist psychology which is an even more severe master than that other enslaver, the annual production of the school play. But in the case of this drawing, we can see a work of art which tells us clearly how important sight is to this boy who cannot hear. We also see a drawing which is a significant success in a disadvantaged life. It is thus a crucial part of this child's PSE, not only as he does it, but also as he is praised for it, as it is displayed and commented upon by the teachers, the nursery nurse and visitors.

Figure 59 *Face*, by boy aged four in black paint

One of the most moving accounts of a disadvantaged child's use of drawing as a means of communication is Lorna Selfe's chapter 'Nadia Chomyn: drawings from 3 to 11 years' in *Six Children Draw* (Payne, 1981). See figures 60 and 61 for examples of Nadia's work. Nadia was diagnosed as autistic when she was very young. To study her drawings is an enriching experience because they show a child with extraordinary visual gifts communicating her perceptions of the world and the pictures she has seen to the world in the best way she can. Her case baffled psychologists and art educationists and intrigued the general public. Her early drawings (at five- to six-years-of-age) show an amazing understanding of proportion and perspective, normally techniques only acquired in adolescence.

Figure 60 *Drawing of a horse*, by Nadia Chomyn, aged five

Figure 61   *Drawing of a horse*, by Nadia Chomyn, aged five

The children at the school described earlier, who experienced behavioural problems, reflected during their project on the relationship between themselves and their parents as they drew, in various media, babies being held. One drawing (figure 58 on page 60) is valuable for its frankness: there was no sniggering as the boy carefully drew the baby's genitals. It is also interesting in the insecure position in which the child is held and in the leaving out of the face. As with the other projects we have mentioned, focusing the children's minds by asking pertinent questions is well worthwhile.

Example questions

- Have you ever held a baby?
- What does it feel like? How did it make you feel?
- What do you think a mother or father feels holding a baby?
- How might the baby feel?
- How do the hands hold the body?
- Look at the eyes; both pairs. Where are they looking? What expressions do they have?
- How are you going to get that effect of light shining there? Of darkness there?
- Can you draw this now from a different angle?

Sometimes art tells us something emotionally without our planning it that way. The sad example in figure C20 on page 111 in the colour section is a painting by a ten-year-old girl of her face. It is surrounded by lurid, clashing colours, amongst which is another face and what might well be an eye. The teacher praised this piece as she felt it deserved recognition, but when she went back to the girl the CND-shaped symbol had been dragged down the face. The teacher told us:

> I said, 'Why have you done that?' and she just burst into tears and ran out of the room. Much later it emerged she'd been being bullied and I think this picture is about that bullying in some way...

This is as eloquent an example as we could hope for to show how art contributes to our education in PSE. The girl used normal communication skills (words) to tell her story but it was her art that opened the floodgates and which brought about the expression.

The following sequence of drawings from a special school (figures 62–70 on pages 68–9) is the outcome of a project to illustrate aspects of school-life for a publication for visitors and parents. The lively involvement and enthusiasm which the children brought to the work is clearly apparent in the unerring directness of the responses.

Figure 62

Figure 63

Figure 64

Figure 65

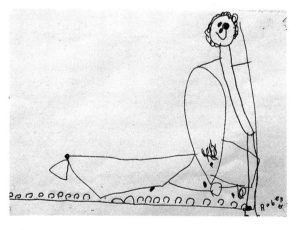

Figure 66

Figure 67

Figure 68

Figure 69

Figure 70

Figures 62–70. Nine drawings, from a special school, illustrating aspects of school life

The three drawings shown below in figures 71, 72 and 73 were made by one eight-year-old boy. The class had listened to Ravel's Bolero and a small group thought it must have something to do with 'old fashioned gypsy music'. Two boys and two girls enjoyed moving and dancing to the music and talked about the kinds of instruments gypsies might have used and what they might wear. The teacher challenged them to get their ideas down in linear form with pens and watered-down paint and to catch the movement and mood. The children were told that they were not to worry if their first experiments did not work, as it was 'really like the page of a sketchbook and not a finished picture'.

Figure 71 *After listening to Ravel's Bolero*

Figure 72 *After listening to Ravel's Bolero*

The boy wasn't pleased with his first attempt but through a process of conversations with the teacher, new efforts and further drafts, he arrived a picture which solved the difficult problem of sitting cross-legged and satisfied him in other, more general ways. There is a build-up of confidence in this work which reinforced the need to teach children to make drafts, not just in writing, but in art too.

The boy's first drawing was the small stilted figure in figure 72, and he was crestfallen by this: 'It doesn't look as if she is dancing'. The development by the end of the session is very striking and only achieved through some sensitive questioning and probing by the teacher: 'Think what it felt like when you were dancing...' This was one session's work.

Figure 73 *After listening to Ravel's Bolero*

Other areas of the curriculum which can have a happy reciprocal relationship with art include physical education (PE) and games. When children are encouraged to draw after a swimming lesson, or a football match, or after a session in the gym, they draw with great vigour if we let them use their work in PE as a stimulus. (See figures 74 and 75 below and figure C21 on page 112 in the colour section.) Religious education also has enormous potential for art, as do history and geography.

We mentioned earlier in this book the importance of surprising children on occasions. One teacher was working with ten-year-olds on a 'time project' and among all the other work with classroom displays of clocks, history books, sundials, calendars and so on, she asked the class to draw a second. That was the stimulus behind the effective but strange uncompleted triangle in light chalks (shown in figure C22 on page 113 in the colour section).

Therefore, while art and design have a right to autonomy in the curriculum, they can help the teaching of other subjects, especially PSE which depends so much on our coming to terms, at least provisionally, with our feelings.

School is about the child's whole life. So is art.

Figure 74 *Doing PE,*
by girl aged six in charcoal

Figure 75 *Doing PE,*
by boy aged six in chalk

5 Looking at faces and heads

THE COHERENT CHILD AND THE FRAGMENTED SYSTEM

We are whole people. This is not an elegant sentence but it conveys an important fact: in our normal functions, in response to whatever life throws at us, we intuitively move freely from one mode of behaviour to another. Sometimes we walk, sometimes we dance, we sing or speak, or make music, enumerate, hypothesise, plan and write.

In curriculum terms, we are dancers, musicians, mathematicians, scientists, technologists and writers and all these elements are part of the whole. One thing might lead to another and we can combine two or more aspects quite naturally, as when we dance and sing with a kind of joy, then flop down and read a book, scribbling (if we are very involved) notes in the margin. This is not integration, which implies an initial separation: it is simply how we are. Human beings do not naturally pigeon-hole themselves. We are coherent, experiencing beings with various ways of expressing our needs, passions, joys and sadness which are all part of the whole business of being ourselves.

The trouble for us adults is that we are old. Over the years we have learnt to separate and disintegrate our experience. Children, on the other hand, instinctively have cohering attitudes and approaches. That is why four-year-olds will unselfconsciously dance to celebrate, naked if the weather allows and then return to painting (their naked bodies, quite possibly), or the telling of the story of why they are happy. We adults have had this ability channelled away from us by various agencies, including our education system and its fragmented approach. We only cohere like this at extreme moments: at weddings and funerals, for example, gazing at ceremonial woundings, or when out of control for some other, usually less honourable, reason.

Of course there is a need to isolate areas of experience in order to consider development and practice but good teachers always seem to be able to re-integrate their own fragmented considerations into a well-structured whole. Indeed, some might argue that really good teachers are coherent in another way: they are the same people in the post office, the pub and the park, as they are in the classroom. Incoherence and disintegration can take us so far away from the ideal of the integrated whole person that we behave like human beings in the park, pub and post office but like teachers at school.

RE-INTEGRATING THE FRAGMENTED SYSTEM USING THE THEME OF FACES AND HEADS

The theme of faces and heads must surely be one of the most basic we could choose that could be explored using any area of the curriculum. To get into the topic we might use a language approach and we might offer the children poetry: a sequence of riddles like this one for instance.

Facing Up: some riddles

I
Pink or dark or gold
with autumn stubble
or pitted with tiny volcanoes,
I prop the rest up.

Or multiplied with age and over-eating
I'm fold after fold of flesh
and sometimes, on a wonder,
nothing.

Lead with me, and oh,
we're both suddenly old.

2
I'm what of yours you've got on him
when he is threatening trouble

And when you have a drink or two
or been hit on the head
I do my work d-double,
I do my work d-double.

3
What a _____ !
You've got a _____ !
And you must turn the other
when you've suffered violence
from sister, friend or brother.
You must be *kind* and *meek* –
then bash them up on Thursday week!

4
Running and blowing
and throwing out rubbish
I'm Greek or Roman,
or quaintly snubbish.

(Fred Sedgwick, (unpublished))

(Answers to the riddle: 1 chin, 2 eye, 3 cheek, 4 nose.)
Children shown riddles like this one quickly catch on to the power of metaphor. For instance, one girl wrote about her freckled nose:

It is covered in light brown petals
and has two passages
that take muck and dust
to history.

Science teachers, by contrast, may approach the subject through the body's structure. The drama and dance teachers will work with expressive faces, arms and hands. The maths teacher will measure. But the child will know, unless led wittingly or unwittingly into fragmented thinking, that a head is a head, and belong to a person or an animal.

If art education is to be a sound part of the whole educational experience, the introductory challenge should enable children to experience valuable work whichever disciplines are involved and whatever the chosen starting point is.

Approaching the theme through art

Portraits

Think for a moment of a portrait you know. It is neither solely a manipulation of paint, or drawing tools, or a superficial photographic likeness. It tells us something and does so through the elements, the emotions and the materials of the artist: in other words, through an integrated range of separate elements.

Artists of all times and cultures have produced portraits which have individual things to say about their subjects and the way in which the artist was thinking or (in the case of some commissioned portraits) what the patron wanted. Children approach such portraits with a lack of experience which in turn generates an openness. They are not impressed by a name, they just know that this is a person who painted or drew and they will say interesting and fresh things. One nine-year-old girl said about Picasso's *Weeping Woman* 'I think he's done how she felt'. A six-year-old boy made the drawing shown in figure 76 after studying the same painting.

Figure 76 *After Picasso's weeping woman*, by boy aged six in pencil

Photographs

Photographic images of old and young people from different ethnic backgrounds in sad and happy moods can be used to support the resources and have much to offer when seen as yet another kind of art. They should not, however, be used as a model to be aimed at in drawing, painting or sculpture.

People and animals

The best resources for drawing are the people around us. Human beings are interested in faces and the human race always has been. Watch a baby follow its parents' eyes around a room. Indeed, animals are equally as interested: look at the dog gazing lovingly, hopefully, droolingly up at its owner's face. Watch a King Charles spaniel control its owner with its eyes on his/her face. Notice how we avoid each others' faces when we are embarrassed.

This interest is illustrated in many of the examples in this book: see especially the work in chapter four on babies and their parents. Four-year-old children show an explorer's interest in their friends', their parents' and their teachers' faces in the work in chapter one. After all, they are still so young, their learning takes huge and coherent strides forward every day. The wonderful drawing on the cover of this book is a superb example of an expressive piece of work based on this topic.

Self-portraits

Self-portraits can be a rich source of quality artwork. Children need mirrors to study closely what they normally see vaguely. Small hand mirrors focused on just a part of the face can lead to some powerful analytical work. Distorted images seen in spoons and tin foil also present useful challenges. As a child draws him/herself, he/she is learning about at least three elements of his/her world: the physiognomy of his/her own face, the tools and materials he/she is using and the relationship between the two which is not always an easy one to handle.

Displays and art galleries

We might build a display of faces, from original artwork wherever possible, or from reproductions of paintings and sculptures and ask children what these and other pictures mean for them. Better still, we

Figure 77   Me, by girl aged four in felt-tip and biro

might visit the National Portrait Gallery or a collection like the one at the Sainsbury Centre at the University of East Anglia in Norwich, which shows us hundreds of pieces of art with a single obsession: the human head. In chapter six we discuss work done after a visit to this gallery, but there is hardly a gallery in the country in which there is not a wealth of art on display which is concerned with the human head, so this work could take place in almost any of them.

Biographies

Another rich resource for work on faces is any biography of, or collection of essays about, the poet W H Auden which contains pictures of his face. (See the list of books at the end of this book.) Auden said his face looked 'like a wedding cake left out in the rain'. We have seen children gazing at photographs of the poet: the sheer difference between their own faces and his evidently mesmerised them and led to some hard thinking and intelligent and sensitive talk. In turn, such work will also lead to good drawing. Most biographies of artists and writers are useful in this way.

Figure 78 *My teacher*, by boy aged four in charcoal

Figure 79 *My friend*, by girl aged four in charcoal

FOCUS ON CHILDREN'S WORK WITH FACES AND HEADS

Looking at themselves

Below and on pages 76 and 77 are some examples of nursery children looking in mirrors, at each other and at their teacher (see also figure C23 on page 114 in the colour section). There is a tension in this work between symbolic depiction and close analysis. For instance the legs may have been shown in a rudimentary symbolic way, while the same child might have gone to some pains to try to solve the problem of depicting the eyebrows, showing close analytical skills. There is also considerable feeling in these drawings.

Figure 80 *Me*, by girl aged four in charcoal

Figure 81 *Miss Williamson*, by girl aged four in felt-tip

Figure 82 *Me in the mirror*, by girl aged four in felt-tip

Looking at black faces

We also found that looking at faces proved to be a way of negating some of the thoughtless prejudice in our society and thus also in our schools. In 'Happy Birthday, Dilroy!', a poem from John Agard's book *I din do nuttin* (1989), Agard depicts a black eight-year-old celebrating his birthday. The boy is having a great birthday, as Susanna Gretz's lively illustrations and the poem both make clear:

> I got a pair of skates
> I want for a long, long time

and he's got lots of cards but there is one thing wrong: why are the little boys on the cards 'so white'? It's hard to think of a better example of our society's casual racism. It only occurred to us when we tried to buy a card for a black child. We can only consider this trivial for an unconsidered moment, until we realise how fundamental a human act celebrating a birthday is.

The main source used for this work based on black faces was Maya Angelou's book *Now Sheba Sings the Song*, which the children had been looking at. The book has stunning illustrations by Tom Feelings and Maya Angelou has dedicated it 'To all my black, brown, beige, yellow, red and white sisters'.

The children looked at the pictures with interest as we encouraged them to examine the drawing techniques, the vigour of the lines and the way in which light and shade had been conveyed to the viewer. The different features of people of varied races set the children a challenge in their drawing. The task of interpreting the images on paper was educational in itself.

Most of the children worked with soft graphite drawing pencils. They had had many opportunities in the past to explore the different kinds of marks a pencil can make and this showed in the ways the children drew the hair, conveying contrasts of light and shade. The black children were particularly pleased to have an opportunity to look at such strong images of their own race. Their drawings, in particular, show a boldness and a willingness to experiment which took our breath away.

Figure 83 *Portrait*, by girl aged ten in pencil

Figure 84 *Drawing of a lady* (after Tom Feelings), by boy aged eleven in pencil

79

Figure 85   *A woman* (after Tom Feelings), by girl aged ten in pencil

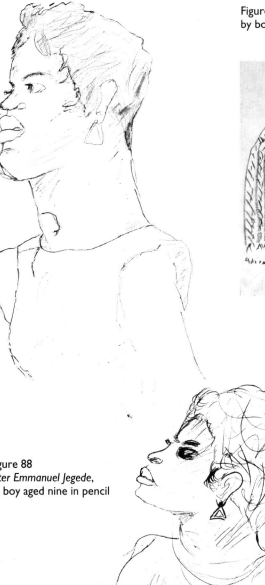

Figure 87   *A lady* (after Tom Feelings), by boy aged ten in blue pastel

Figure 86   *Head* (after Tom Feelings), by boy aged ten in felt-tip (running out)

Figure 88
After Emmanuel Jegede, by boy aged nine in pencil

Figure 89   *Lady with earrings* (after Tom Feelings), by girl aged eleven in blue pencil

Figure 90   *The man is covering his mouth (after Emmanuel Jegede), by girl aged six in pencil*

Raised consciousness in these terms can be achieved by employing a writer in residence like Emmanuel Jegede, the Nigerian poet, artist, and musician, or Winston Lewis, the drummer and storyteller. You can also make sure that you use published material which gives an appropriate balance to ethnic minorities, such as Fred Sedgwick's anthology of poems for children, *This Way That Way*, which was designed to offer all children a presence in the books which they came across.

Materials and styles

During this project we offered the older children a choice of materials: drawing pencil, blue chalk, charcoal and ballpoint pens. Each of these materials set them interesting problems. The marks produced by the ballpoints, for example, cannot be erased and therefore the mistakes have to stay. This fact is useful in teaching children that lines which seem wrong can be interesting, or are naturally ignored. Very often this variety of lines creates a liveliness and movement that is not there otherwise. The ballpoints influence children away from the cartoonish, photographic way of drawing which insists so tediously on exactness.

This cartoon influence can be seen in figure 91. We have included it for two reasons: firstly to illustrate a clichéd way of looking which often displays a lack of depth and secondly because, on a more positive note, it possesses a humour which we need to encourage in our schools. In the context of guiding children away from erasing and a preoccupation with exactness we also show them drawings by artists as varied as Nadia Chomyn, Shirley Hughes, Picasso, Giacometti and Leonardo da Vinci, all of whom use a variety of lines, none of which is the only 'right' one.

Figure 91   *Man with glasses, by boy aged nine in pencil*

Some children in this age group, ten- to eleven-years-of-age, don't like charcoal as a material because it seems messy and they're at a stage when precise photographic images are the objectives of their drawing. However, they should be encouraged to use it because it helps them to understand the value of process: the pleasure to be had from handling a material which is scratchy and imprecise. The same can be said about the chalk.

After we had given the children a choice of materials and they had finished a drawing, we offered them the opportunity to do another piece using a different material and studying a different page in the Angelou book. Sometimes we took away a drawing which the child felt wasn't finished: 'That's lovely – now do another one'. This was partly to capture a powerful image which might have been lost in further work, but also to teach the children not to be too holy about art. It can be something that you practise, on occasions, with quick strokes. It is part of life and not something to be idolised. One of the drawings which was done in this way is the head showing the right profile in a black felt-tip pen which is running out (figure 86 on page 80). This remarkable image was the work of a ten-year-old boy who drew it in about three minutes.

Figure 93 *African mask and Peruvian pipe*, by girl aged ten in pencil, charcoal and fine felt-tip

Figure 92 *African mask*, by girl aged four in white paint

Above all, art can help us to celebrate our common humanity, whatever colour or sex we are. All the world's varied cultures and people draw and always have done. We can learn about other peoples' lives and ways of seeing through their art.

Younger children

The benefits of this project can also be achieved with very young children. Four-year-olds were shown examples of African art, including masks, and they drew pictures like the large white drawing in thick paint on black paper (see figure 92). It was important that these young children had the experience of working on a large scale in drawing. The scale can be increased with older children by fixing the brushes to wooden batons and getting the children to draw, effectively, with graphic tools which are three feet long. This loosens children up remarkably because they are working from the shoulder with the whole arm, rather than with the fingers and wrists only. Other older children in a drawing club have studied African masks and a tiny Peruvian smoking pipe in the form of an ear-ringed human figure holding a cooking bowl (figures 93, 94 and 95).

Figure 94   *African mask*, by girl aged ten in variety of pencils

Figure 95   *Mexican statue* (large head), and *Peruvian God statue*, by boy aged ten in pencil and charcoal

Looking both ways

Another way of approaching the drawing of faces is to set up a mirror at an angle to the face. This means the child has to look in one direction to draw (at the paper) and in a very different one to study her face (at a mirror placed to one side). This in turn sets an interesting challenge and implicitly teaches us that there is more than one way of looking at anything, even one's own face. It makes the child draw his/her eyes very expressively. The work begins to resemble the work of Picasso, where he breaks images up and looks at them simultaneously from two or even three different positions.

The following questions are some which we asked children when we were examining faces. We first asked them to look carefully through a book of good reproductions or, better still, some relevant original work and then asked them:

Figure 96 *Self-portrait,* by boy aged ten in pencil

Example questions

- What is the shape of the nose, eyes and mouth like?
- Tell me some words to do with colour which would describe the particular face that you are looking at.
- What is the texture of the face?
- What does it feel like?
- What does the texture and look of the skin remind you of?
- How do old faces and young faces differ?
- What makes the expression change?
- Can you describe the expression in the eyes and the mouth?
- What does the pattern and texture of the hair remind you of?

Figure 97 *Self-portrait,* by boy aged nine in pencil

Aural influences

The girl who painted the rock group in figure C24 on page 115 in the colour section, has experienced another angle on this subject. She briefly saw the cover of a record but the main stimulus for this picture was aural. Her teacher told us:

I played rock records very loudly: Pink Floyd, Rolling Stones, stuff they'd brought in . . . we were lucky then because we had a mobile classroom which was separate from the rest of the school and you could make almost as much noise as you liked and I'd got permission to make it into an art room. Well, I played the records very loudly indeed and the children thought it was great and so did I. . . And then I said, get that noise on the paper, record that sound visually. What colours are those guitars, those drums? And where do rock groups play? What expressions are on their faces? Have you seen any live rock groups? Think of television programmes you've seen with rock groups on. Get your favourite groups into your mind, look at them with your mind's eye. . . How are you going to get the sheer noise on to the paper? The rhythm? How are you going to put the paint on? You must use at least one way apart from brushes. And then I put the music on again and watched them paint.

Drama as an incentive

Figure 98 *Large puppets, by eight- to eleven-year-olds, in foam rubber, wire, fabric*

Another school had these extraordinary huge puppets in a classroom (see figure 98). They were made by the children and used in a production of *East of the Sun and West of the Moon*, a play the teacher wrote based on the frog prince story. Each puppet required three children to work it and this presented interesting problem-solving challenges. The thinking and the reasoning must have been extremely complex for the play to run as smoothly as it did. Once the play was over the puppets became interesting features of the classroom. They are made of foam rubber, tissue-paper, cane, polystyrene and the headteacher's waste paper basket, which forms one of the heads.

CONCLUSION

We have filled this chapter with images firstly because they are exciting but also because they show that there are many more ways of making marks than one might initially think of. (See figures C25–C31 on pages 116–119 in the colour section for more examples of faces and heads.)

6 Using art

The National Curriculum requirement which states:

> pupils should understand art in a variety of genres and styles from a variety of cultures, Western and non-Western . . .

is not an alien concept to many teachers. Much good work has already been done in this area and has been supported by books such as Rod Taylor's *Education for Art*. Likewise, in her book *Art 4–11*, Margaret Morgan says that:

> the purpose of introducing children to the experience of art and design forms is two-fold: first as a means of inspiring interest and enjoyment . . . and second to extend expectations with regard to art and design. . .

This work cannot begin without a school building up basic resources and constantly adding to and evaluating them. The resources we are concerned with here are originals, reproductions, books and artists, designers and craftspeople working in schools.

Reproductions

The easiest (although not the most effective) way to help children become familiar with art is for a school to buy prints, posters, good books of reproductions and postcards and to also keep an eye open for art in those newspapers with colour supplements. The Saturday edition of *The Independent,* for example, nearly always has excellently produced art. One week the paper may reproduce one of the Impressionists, another week it will feature some more challenging Modernists. Similarly, the subject matter can range from fine art, through to computer art, photography and advertising, to folk and decorative art.

The technology which has made reproductions easily and cheaply available has democratised art in our century and we should be grateful for this. It is strange to reflect that although the wealthy characters in Austen's novels had never heard Mozart play, or seen Michelangelo's work in any form at all, children in many primary schools are surrounded by reproductions of art and frequently hear the music of the world's most talented composers and musicians.

Originals

However it is, of course, even better to see art and design forms firsthand. Although reproductions potentially bring art to all of us, they also notoriously cheapen the experience. Reproductions make large canvases smaller and destroy the three-dimensional effect of sculpture. The photographic quality of finishes also varies in quality. They also teach us very little about how a composition is built-up, as reproductions usually destroy the evidence of, for example, texture and brushstrokes.

Most importantly, however, reproductions diminish art's effect simply by being reproductions: they militate against our understanding of the uniqueness of each piece of art. At worst they make of art something little better than the top of a chocolate box, as when Monet scenes are disempowered, and reduced to no more than a background image of a picnic. A friend of ours calls this the 'poppies-in-the-corn' effect of reproductions. This works against the educational, transforming power of art by making it merely decorative.

Artists in residence

Originals, therefore, are far preferable. There are several ways of helping children to gain the experience of seeing original art. One is to have an artist or an art student in residence. The advantage of this is that the children can see the art being made. They see the commitment of the artist to the materials and the subject and they see ways of organising often messy materials efficiently. They can also talk and listen as the process goes on. Fred Sedgwick's books *Here Comes the Assembly Man* (1989) and *The Expressive Arts* (1993) both contain accounts of artists working with primary school children. The schools concerned found some of the funding at their local Arts Association and it is always worth trying to tap sources like this.

Borrowing originals

Another way is to borrow original works of art. Some authorities have collections which schools can use. Otherwise, some artists will lend their pictures and sculptures and time and effort spent in getting to know artists living near the school is more than well spent.

Galleries and museums

Most towns have art galleries and museums which offer free admission and schools which acquire the habit of visiting them find the quality of the children's work improves dramatically. Some galleries also put on travelling exhibitions. The clipboards which children bring to these galleries do not contain questions, but blank sheets of paper on which they respond to the work around them by sketching and making notes.

WHAT CHILDREN GAIN FROM LOOKING AT ART

Children gain two huge advantages from looking at art. The first is that they learn about their heritage, whether that heritage is national or, preferably, worldwide. For this they need to see as wide a variety of art, craft and design as possible, so that their working definitions are flexible and generous. The second gain is to their own artwork and working methods. Obviously, children who have examined other art forms will work with greater knowledge of technique (provided they have been led to consider how the work was done) and a greater openness to what their graphic tools can do, whether these tools are brushes, crayons, pencils, batik or modelling tools.

Children's work – using a portrait gallery

A group of eight-, nine- and ten-year-old children visited the Sainsbury Centre at the University of East Anglia in Norwich. This gallery is an extraordinarily coherent collection because it represents and displays the taste of just two people, Sir Robert and Lady Sainsbury. It contains a first century BC figure of a mother goddess from north-west India and sculptures by the disturbing artist John Davies (born 1946) as well as much in between. The coherence is created by the fact that through it all there is an obsession with the human head.

To walk around this collection is to learn a great deal about what it is to be human today as well as about what our forebears were like. It shows us what it was like to be a worshipping, creating, thinking human throughout the past and all over the globe. Here there is no mean-spirited obsession with our European heritage in isolation. For the Sainsburys, a Yoruba working during the last century is of as much interest as Henry Moore working in this one.

All the children were impressed by one or more of the pieces on show there and the security staff were also impressed by the children's mature responses to the art. We would like to reiterate a point we have made elsewhere: a school has to develop its own tradition in art. Mature, critical responses do not come out of nothing one wet Wednesday, but develop from the school's micro-tradition of honouring art and its power to teach.

One girl looked for a long time at painting by Francis Bacon. A boy stared for ages at a Graeco–Roman head before returning to school to produce the multi-media drawing on the cover of this book. He found a piece of white paper that had been used by another child to clean paint from a roller and then built up a design in pastels (see figure C32 on page 120 in the colour section). 'How did you come to choose that particular piece of paper?' we asked him, and the answer was a blank face and a shrug. 'I suspect' the classroom helper said, 'it was luck . . .' And of course luck does play a part, with inspiration and sheer hard work, in the making of art. His teacher told us that a member of his staff had said how watching this boy draw:

> made the hairs on the back of your neck prickle . . . he starts anywhere, an ear for example, and just draws, just goes on, it's frightening to watch. . .

The same boy also drew the head in black ink (see figure 99), while looking at a book of reproductions. In this piece of work the massive variety of his graphic experience has paid off in a different way.

Figure 99 *Head*, by boy aged nine in black ink

Children's work – using a resident artist

Children at another school worked with the artist Saleem Arif. A teacher made a frame from a sheet of A4 paper and asked the child to choose a piece of one of Arif's canvases which interested her. She moved the frame around the glass, covering the picture until she found the section which interested her most, then she stuck the paper on to the glass in the appropriate position. This not only concentrated her eyes and her mind but also increased her sense of security: she no longer had the whole large picture to worry about, just part of it. The result was the drawing 'Snake Man' (see figure 100). Because of the varied uses of pencil and because of the exercise with the frame, this piece has movement and vitality as well as a little mystery. Similarly, two pieces of work were generated by another artist's residency using the same technique. This time the artist was the Nigerian Emmanuel Jegede and both the children had framed part of one of Jegede's pictures. Again they were asked to isolate the part of the picture which they found most interesting, put a paper frame round it and then to study it. They then drew it, and wrote a poem (see figures C33 and C34 on pages 121–2 in the colour section).

Children's work – using an art workshop

At another school a group of children were taken by bus to Wingfield College in Suffolk. The night before the visit was one of the wildest that Suffolk had known for years and there was an air of excitement among the children as they discussed the fallen or broken trees and how some had been bent nearly double by the wind. The building itself was once a medieval college for training ordinands and was also later the home of the Duke of Suffolk, whose wife was Henry VIII's sister, Mary Rose, after whom the famous but fated ship was named. This fact caused much animated discussion. The house stands alongside a fourteenth-century church and in the grounds there are modern sculptures. The site was therefore full of historical and artistic interest.

The theme of the project was story-making. Teachers and children worked with a musician, a writer, a storyteller, a dancer, a toymaker, an environmentalist, a museums officer and the artist, illustrator and painter Antony Maitland.

Antony Maitland's group worked on the floor of the great hall where there was a collection of his work and books that he had illustrated on show. The children later moved into the church. He spoke to them about getting back to the life of the people and the building in the past by using their imaginations and the need to carry out research. Meanwhile he was drawing, showing the children the kind of processes he worked through. Figure C35, on page 123 in the colour section shows the children's drawings of the windblown trees, the church and the house, as well as some of their writings.

Figure 100 *Snake-man* (after Saleem Arif), by girl aged nine in pencil

Children's work – using reproductions

Despite our earlier remarks about the problems which surround using reproductions, these examples of children's work produced after looking at reproductions of Lowry paintings show that it can be a successful method (see figures 101–3). The children were four-years-old and the teacher asked them where they thought all the people in the pictures were going. Their answers were very wide-ranging and included: for a walk; to their houses; up the pub; to Felixstowe; to Sainsburys; to catch a bus; this way and that way; to the bank; shopping, because some have bags; or that they were waiting for a boat; going to church; or to feed the ducks.

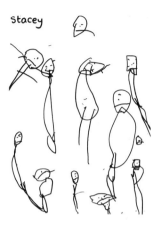

Figure 101 *After Lowry reproductions*, by girl aged four in felt-tip

Figure 102 *After Lowry reproductions*, by boy aged four in charcoal and felt-tip

Asking the children to talk as they look at pictures is a way of intensifying their experience of art. Other questions we might ask them as they look at, for example, Lowry's work are:

Figure 103 *After Lowry reproductions*, by girl aged four in charcoal and felt-tip

Example questions

- What do you think of it?
- How does it make you feel? Why?
- What sort of mood does this picture have?
- Why is the sky that colour? How do you think he mixed it?
- What do you think is in that building?
- What is that huge wheel for?
- What time of day do you think it is?

An eleven-year-old boy looked at reproductions of work by Klee. His picture (see figure C36 on page 125 in the colour section) was made largely with sponges dipped in powder paint and charcoal. It is hard to over-estimate the depth of the learning that has gone on here. He has looked at Klee's work, enjoyed it, and thought deeply about it. He has gone through the complicated mental and imaginative procedures involved in using another artist's insights in his own work. He has then learnt about the skills required in making a work of art of his own. A ten-year-old girl looked at Blake's painting of Nebuchadnezzar and made the print in figure 104 (which she sold to us, in the spirit of the times, for fifty pence). Another girl, aged nine, worked from Picasso's *Lady with a Red Hat*, using powder paint and then cut it up and rearranged it after a discussion with her teacher about Picasso's cubist work (see figure C37 on page 126 in the colour section).

Figure 104 *After Blake's Nebuchadnezzar*, by girl aged ten in Lino print

Children's work – using their own experiences

In another school we found a ceramic fox on display in the assembly hall. The headteacher told us that it had been awarded as The Schools' Curriculum Award by the Department of Education and Science for excellent curriculum work by the school. He also told us that about the same time that the award was made, one class saw a real fox stalking around the school grounds. Their class-teacher had then read the class a story about a fox and the children had used the sighting as a basis for some work on foxes:

> **First we did those pencil drawings [see figure 105] and we talked a lot about foxes, looked them up, looked at the ceramic and so on ... then they wrote poems like this one by a seven-year-old:**

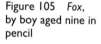

> A sharp pointed face
> Moved in the garden,
> Leaping swiftly through the grass,
> His tail like a brush,
> His fur like gold,
> His face like an arrow.
> He starts to walk.
> He develops into a run.
> He disappears into the trees
> Never to be seen again.

Figure 105   *Fox,* by boy aged nine in pencil

> **Then we did drawings with those crayons you dip in water [water colour pencils, or aquarelles – see figure C38 on page 127 in the colour section], it was the first time they'd seen them, we were experimenting really ... Then we did the fox in batik ... [see figure C39 on page 128 in the colour section].**

It has become fashionable to mistrust what has been called 'the dead pigeon curriculum', by which critics mean lessons which depend on a sudden inspiration, a sudden startling dramatic event: a dead bird in the playground, a thunderstorm, or fire engines congregating outside on the street. But we might ask what one is to do when these events take place. Should teacher and children have ignored the fox and its prowling and got on with whatever that term's topic was deemed to be, the Victorians, movement, space? Surely not. The learning which takes place after something as remarkable as this has occurred is bound to be powerful if it taps the children's excitement. As this work shows, it extends over several curriculum areas: art, of course, science and language.

At such a time our job as teachers is to guide the learning that has spontaneously arisen and to find it a place in the context of the National Curriculum. One can be sure that if the process through which learners go is an engaging one, it will have a place in a rationally designed curriculum.

Another striking element in this work is the quality of the materials the children have worked with. The paper, for example, is cartridge. The pencils are of a high quality and there is a variety of other graphic tools around, even extending to wax resist. This teaches the children something vital. If we imply that art doesn't matter by giving the children third-rate, cheap materials, we are teaching them that it is less important than, for example, mathematics, where the graph paper is the real thing, not off-cuts from the local paper factory.

Other children looked at a large bronze of a dog and made chalk and felt-tip drawings of it, an example of which can be seen in figure 106 below.

Figure 106 *Dog* (after looking at a large bronze sculpture), by boy aged seven in felt-tip

The following example questions are some which we might ask children as they look at a work of art:

Example questions

- How do you think the artist has done that?
- Why do you suppose he/she has chosen this subject? (This looks at the vital question of the artist's relationship with the subject matter.)
- Why do you think he/she chose to use, for example, pencil instead of paint or pastel?
- What shapes can you find in this picture?
- Can you find different ways in which the pen or pencil or brush has been used?
- What different colours can you find? Why has the artist used these particular colours?
- How do you think this person (in the picture) feels about things going on around her?
- How has this man's hair been painted? And the clouds?

CONCLUSION

Whether at one level children are working from reproductions, or whether at a very different level they are working from original works or with an artist, they gain a valuable insight into what it is to be human from looking at art. Studying a work of art is a direct, non-verbal experience and potentially an exciting and educational one which involves thinking, feeling and reasoning. There is no need for critics and art historians to come between the child and his/her response: children are excellent critics themselves, given the necessary experience.

In the same way, when children study art forms intensively, they understand more about what it is to be an artist: a human being who expresses his/her humanity by making things in order to try to understand the world and the artist's place in it. While we will not, of course, all be great artists, we all have the right to draw those lines which are lines into knowledge, which are a kind of thinking aloud. It is irrelevant whether that thinking is by early humankind worrying about its next meal, or some complex reflection on a canvas by Paul Klee, or that other artist, the one who lives down the road.

List of books referred to by the authors

Agard, John. 'Happy Birthday, Dilroy!' in *I din do nuttin*, London, Bodley Head, 1989

Angelou, Maya. *Now Sheba Sings the Song*, London, Virago, 1987

Carpenter, Humphrey. *W H Auden*, London, Allen and Unwin, 1981

Causley, Charles. 'When I was a boy' in *Early in the Morning*, London, Kestrel, 1987

Farnan, Dorothy, J. *Auden In Love*, London, Faber and Faber, 1984

Herbert, George. *The Poems*, Oxford, Oxford University Press, 1961

Jackson, Margaret. *Display and Environment for Learning*, Sevenoaks, Hodder and Stoughton, 1993

Johnson, Paul. *Literacy and the Book Arts*, Sevenoaks, Hodder and Stoughton, 1992

Mary Glasgow Publications. *Topic Support Packs*, London, Mary Glasgow Publications, 1989

Matisse, Henri. *Jazz*, Paris, Teriade, 1947

Morgan, Margaret. *Art 4–11*, Oxford, Blackwells, 1988; London, Simon and Schuster, 1992

National Curriculum Council, *National Curriculum documents 1989–1992*, London, Department of Education and Science, the Welsh Office

Newland, Mary and Rubens, Maurice. *Some Functions of Art in the Primary School*, London, ILEA, 1984

Osborne, Charles. *W H Auden. The Life of a Poet*, London, Eyre Methuen, 1980

Payne, Shiela. *Six Children Draw*, London, Academic Press, 1981

Rawson, Philip. *Seeing Through Drawing*, London, BBC, 1979

Schools Council – Art Working Party, *Art 7–11*, Schools Council, London, 1978

Sedgwick, Fred. *Here Comes the Assembly Man*, Basingstoke, Falmer, 1989

Sedgwick, Fred. *The Expressive Arts*, London, David Fulton, 1993

Sedgwick, Fred. *Pizza, Curry, Fish and Chips,* Harlow, Longman, to be published 1994

Sedgwick, Fred. *This Way That Way*, London, Mary Glasgow Publications, 1989

Spender, Stephen. *W H Auden. A Tribute selected by Stephen Spender*, London, Weidenfeld and Nicholson, 1975

Tanner, Robin. Address to Wiltshire teachers, advisors and ex-pupils, Wiltshire, unpublished, 1984

Taylor, Rod. *Education for Art*, Harlow, Longman, 1986

Colour section – children's art from one to eleven years

Figure C1   *First Marks*, by girl aged one in felt-tips

Figure C2   *Kelly on a swing*, by girl in paint

97

Figure C3   *We all had a bath*, by girl aged five in pencil and crayon

Figure C4   *We all had a bath*, by boy aged five in pencil and crayon

the owl
looks
Real
it
fathers
feel
soft
as
silk
it
claws
are
Sharp
It
eyes
Glow

By
VICKI

The owl is like a man whiteing for a thign.
It look so Reall
los chaws are kifes

Figure C5 *Owl*, by girl aged nine in pencil, coloured pencils and biro

Figure C6 *Owl*, by boy aged nine in pencils and black ink

Figure C7   *Plant,* by girl aged nine in paint

Figure C8   *Sea,* by boy aged ten in paint

Figure C9   *Spider plant*, by girl aged ten in paint

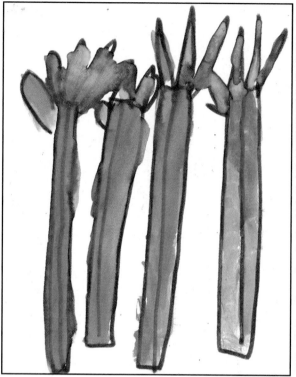

Figure C10 (a) and (b) *Drawings from the supermarket*, by a group in paint and crayon

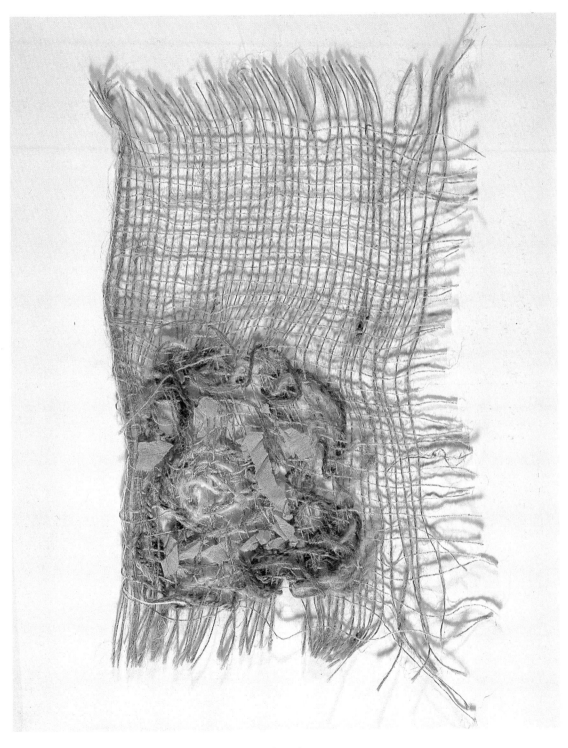

Figure C11   *Weaving,* by girl aged ten in wool, paper, thread

Figure C12 *Collage*, by girl aged ten in torn paper

Figure C13   *Collage*, by girl aged ten in torn paper

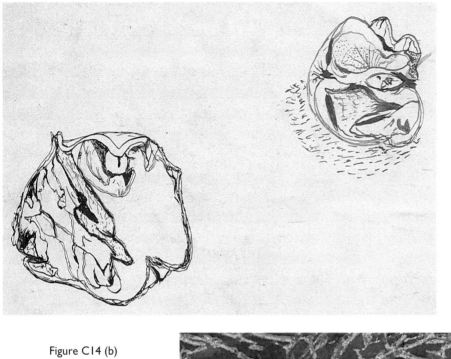

Figure C14 (a)

Figure C14 (b)

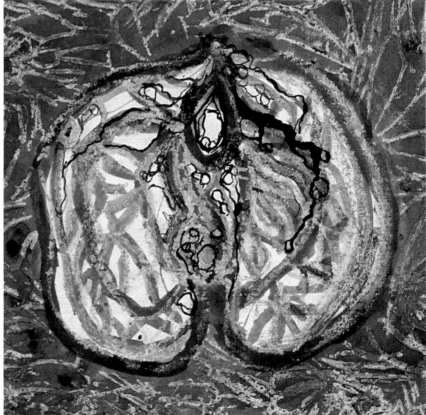

Figure C14 (a, b, c, d, e) *Studies for nut collages*, by girl aged eleven in pencil, pen and ink, and wax resist

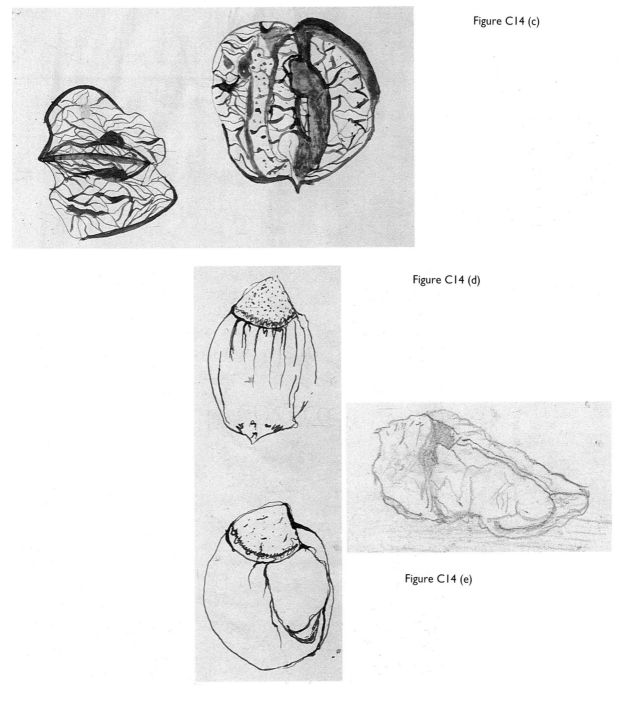

Figure C14 (c)

Figure C14 (d)

Figure C14 (e)

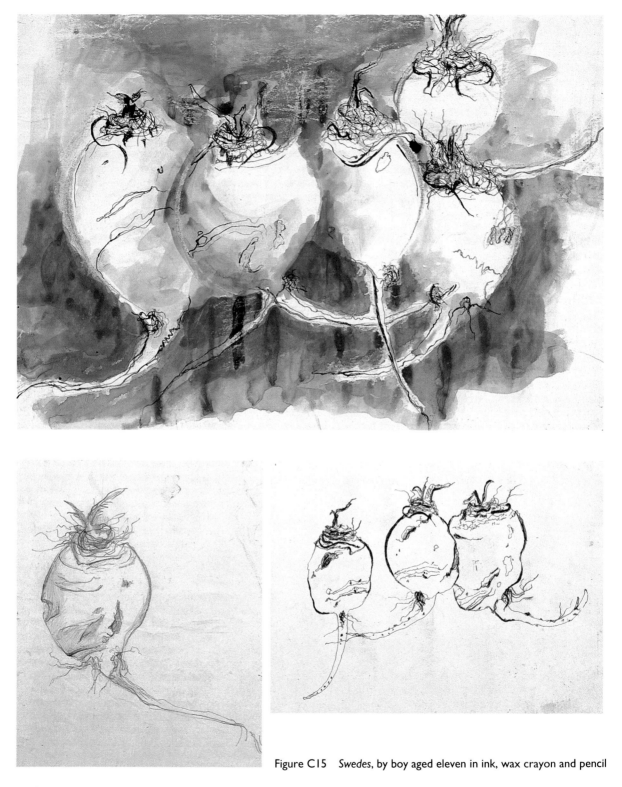

Figure C15 *Swedes*, by boy aged eleven in ink, wax crayon and pencil

Figure C16 *Bike*, by girl aged eight in pencil and felt-tip

Figure C17 *Part of a bike*, in paint

Figure C18 *Bike*, by girl aged eight in pencil and felt-tip

Figure C19 *Mother and child*, by boy aged nine in pencil, pastel and paint

Figure C20   *My face*, by girl aged ten in paint

Figure C21 *After playing football*, by boy aged eleven in paint

Figure C22 *A second*, by girl aged ten in chalks

Figure C23 *Ourselves*, by nursery-aged children in felt-tips

Figure C24 *Rock group*, by girl aged eleven in paint and chalk

Figure C25   *A woman smoking*, by two girls aged ten in paint/marvin medium

Figure C26 *Face collage*, by girl aged seven in tissue paper, pipe cleaners and various fabrics

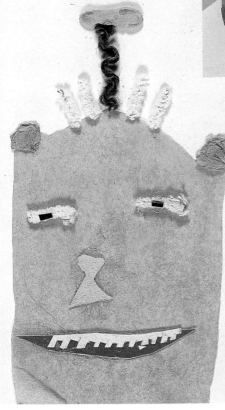

Figure C27 *Face collage*, by girl aged seven in tissue paper, wool, blue-tak, card and pipe cleaners

Figure C28 *People*, by boy aged nine in paint

Figure C29 *Singers*, by girl aged nine in paint

Figure C30   *Faces*, by girl aged seven in paint

Figure C31   *Three-dimensional head*, by boy
aged eight in papier mâchè, paint, fur

Figure C32   *After Graeco–Roman head*, by boy aged ten in inks, pastels, chalks

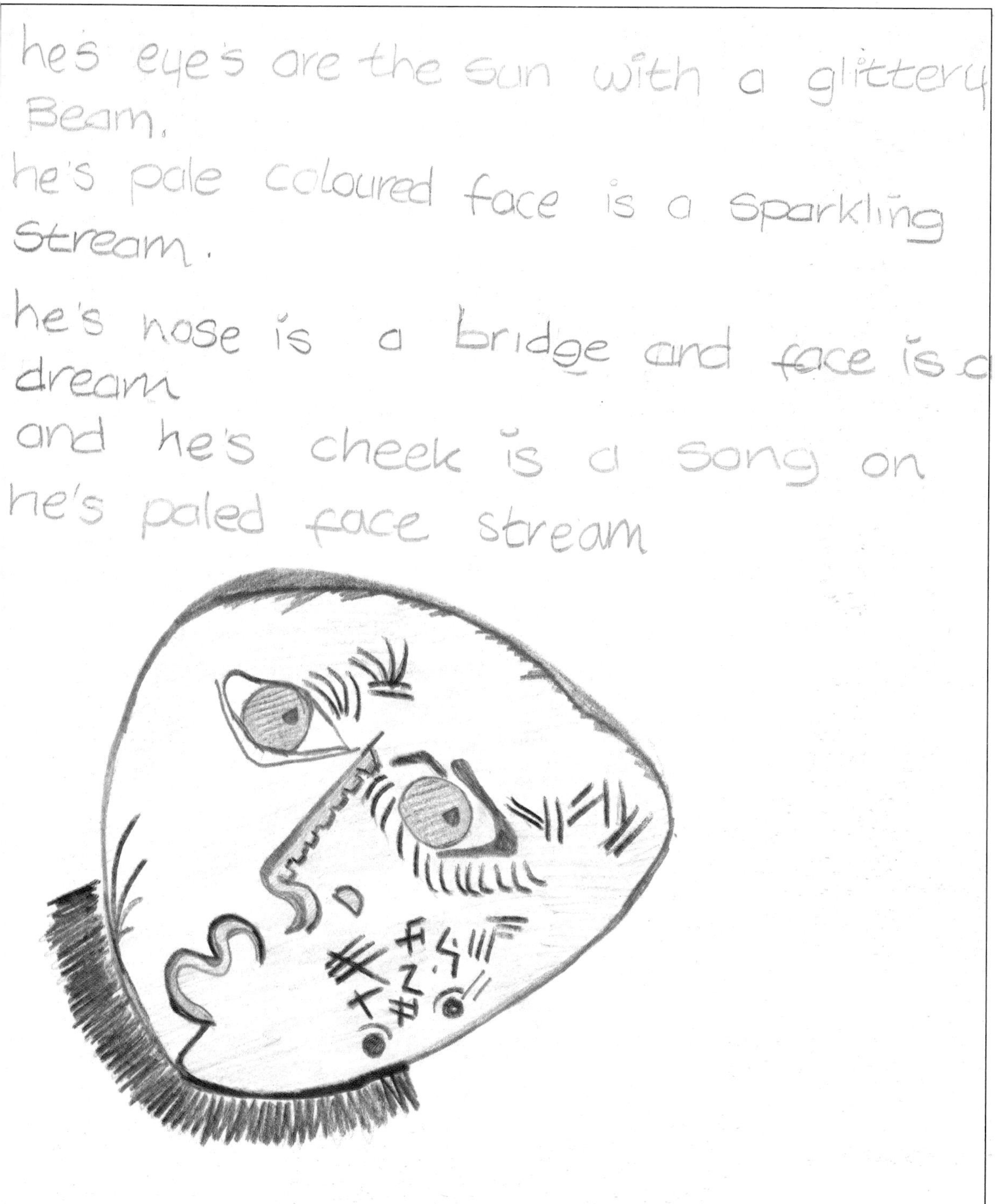

he's eye's are the sun with a glittery
Beam,
he's pale coloured face is a Sparkling
Stream.

he's nose is a bridge and face is a
dream
and he's cheek is a song on
he's paled face stream

Figure C33 *His eyes are the sun* (after Emmanuel Jegede), by girl aged eleven in pencil

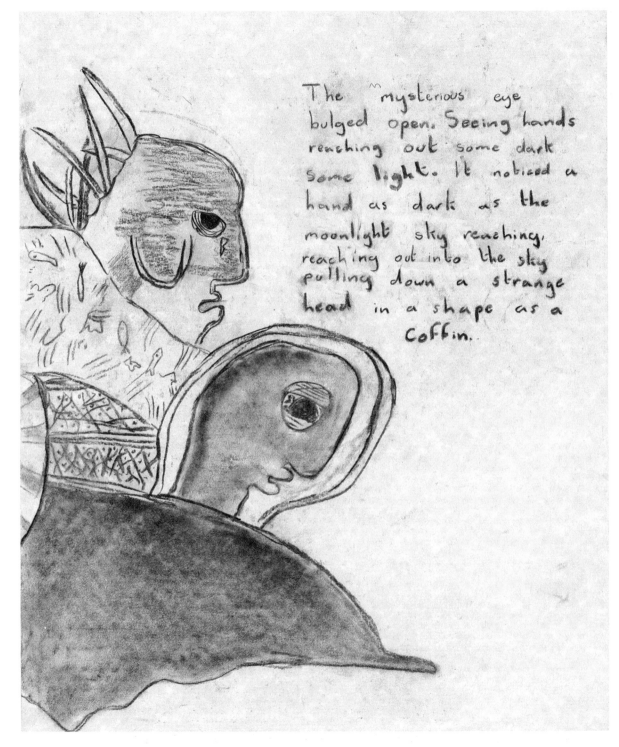

The mysterious eye bulged open. Seeing hands reaching out some dark some light. It noticed a hand as dark as the moonlight sky reaching, reaching out into the sky pulling down a strange head in a shape as a coffin.

Figure C34   *After Emmanuel Jegede*, by boy aged ten in charcoal

Figure C35(a)

Figure C35(b)

Figure C35   (a)–(i)
(here and overleaf)
*Children working
with Antony Maitland,
artist in residence
at Wingfield
College*

Figure C35(c)

Figure C35(d)

Figure C35(e)

Figure C35(f)

Figure C35(g)

Figure C35(i)

Figure C35(h)

Figure C36   *After Paul Klee*, by boy aged eleven in charcoal and powder paint (applied with sponges)

Figure C37　*After Picasso*, by girl aged nine in powder paint

Figure C38   *Fox*, by girl aged ten in pencil and 'aquarelles' (water-colour pencils)

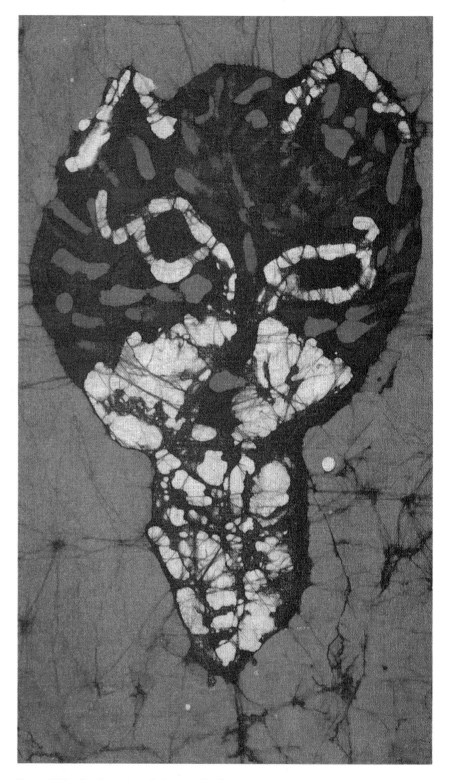

Figure C39   *Fox*, by girl aged eleven in batik